SECRETS BEHIND THE BURQA

Secrets Behind The Burqa

Published by Isaac Publishing 6729 Curran Street, McLean VA 22101
Copyright © 2008 Rosemary Sookhdeo

First US edition: May 2008
First published in the United Kingdom by Isaac Publishing 2004
Reprinted 2005 and 2006

All quotations from the Qur'an except otherwise stated are from "The Meaning
of the Glorious Qur'an" translated by Mohammad Marmaduke Pickthall
(Birmingham:UK Islamic Mission Dawah Centre 1997)

All quotations from the Hadith The Alim, (Silver Springs, Maryland US: ISL
Software Corp. 1986-99)

ISBN 978-0-9787141-4-7

Printed in the United States of America

SECRETS BEHIND THE BURQA

ROSEMARY SOOKHDEO

Isaac Publishing
McLean VA

Contents

Introduction

In 1970 after theological college, my husband and I embarked on a ministry amongst the Muslim community in Britain. For five years we travelled the length and breadth of Britain presenting the needs and the challenge of reaching Muslims, to churches across all denominations. We conducted training seminars on how to understand Islam and the Muslim in our midst. In some areas we spent several months, and worked together with other organisations involved in the same work. At the end of the five years we were very disillusioned and disheartened by the lack of interest in the British churches and the antagonism and racism we had experienced. We found people were very fearful of what seemed the great unknown. It was only with the individual person here and there that we had found any interest at all. It was out of this disillusionment and what seemed the futility of our task, that we took the decision to settle down in an inner city area and pioneer a work ourselves.

During these five years I visited many Muslim homes and grew to understand Islamic culture and the women's role and position within the family and home. I spent many hours with Muslim women in very much a learning situation. I realised very quickly that I could only have relationships with the women and girls, as relationships across the sexes were not acceptable in Islamic culture.

It was in 1975 that my husband and I formed an organisation

called In Contact Ministries (later to be renamed Servants Fellowship International) and purchased the St Andrew's Centre in Plaistow, East London, a very large redundant complex, with the specific aim of ministering to the Muslim and other ethnic communities in the area. In 1975 the Muslim community in Newham numbered 15,000; today it is 58,500.[1] The non-white community in the area is now 60.6%, which is the highest of any borough in Britain.[2] With a staff of over forty at times, we taught English as a foreign language, started a drop-in centre for those who wanted help in various areas such as filling in DHSS forms, took people to hospital for their appointments, conducted a refugee ministry supplying furniture and physical needs, and a crisis pregnancy centre, amongst other things. Over the years many Muslim people were visited in their homes. We offered friendship to help overcome their loneliness and often depression, and had many discussions in Muslim homes on the differences between Islam and Christianity.

Although our main burden was for the Muslim community we ended up in ministering to any person who came across our path, including those from the other faith communities, believing that they had been sent by God. Thus the church that was planted was a multiracial church, and today has some 28 nationalities.

The Context-The East End Of London

The context in which we worked is that of Plaistow in East London, which is in the borough of Newham and was historically a white working class area. It was in the 1950s, with the advent of immigration that many West Indians and Asians moved into the area, the majority of Asians being from the Muslim community in Pakistan. It was as the non-white community moved in that the white community began to move out. As a result the various communities began to form pockets within the area, which we see to this day. It is not uncommon to see one side of a street almost totally Hindu, while the other side is Muslim. The majority of the Muslims who moved into the area came from the poorest classes in society and from the rural areas. Those that were educated found it almost impossible to find work in the area of their training and had to accept any work they could get. This often meant working in the factories such as Ford in Dagenham. The Muslim community did not have its structures in place as it has today, and there were only a few house-mosques in the area.

It was in the ensuing years that many in the Muslim community started small businesses and became wealthy. All members of the family would be involved in the business, including the women, and would work long hours to be successful. With this came the desire to educate their children with the aim that they would become doctors, solicitors and lawyers. They wanted the best for their children and would sacrifice to educate them. However in many cases this would apply only to members of the male sex. Thus a new middle class arose. Interestingly enough, today the private schools in the area, including the Christian ones have many Muslims attending them. Today the Muslim community is well established in Newham with newly built mosques and many shops including their own bookshops.

Over the 23 years we lived in the area we saw Newham change from an area of extreme deprivation to an area that, in the latter part of eighties, became desirable for the young white middle class professional. Many moved into the area. However in the mid-nineties we saw the exodus of these self-same people. Newham was rapidly increasing its non-white population with large numbers of refugees. It became one of the two main receiving boroughs in Great Britain, and every year accepted between ten and twenty thousand refugees who lived in hotels and every place where it was possible to house them in bed and breakfast accommodation. The area became poorer once again, until it was designated the poorest area in Britain. The ethnic diversity of the population grew, with the proportion of non-white residents reaching 52%. Muslims who had made sufficient money moved to outlying 'better class areas' such as Ilford and further East into Essex.

As these changes took place within the community and the next generation was born in this country, Muslim young people began to exhibit the individualism of their English peers and society at large. Parents found it hard to understand what was happening. Young people were growing up in two cultures, and this brought tension and conflict between generations. It was at around this time that more Muslim women started going out to work, for economic reasons: to help establish the family (house prices were rising fast), and to make as much money as possible in what was considered a land of plenty. Cultural patterns were beginning to change.

The Motivation

Called by God, my husband and I went to the East End of London to work amongst the stranger and the alien. I lived there for the majority of my adult life, and it became my context both pastorally and theologically. I was born and brought up in New Zealand, so in the East End I felt very much a stranger and an alien in a foreign land. I was different from many other foreign-born residents in that I was white, that set me apart, but my husband is Asian so was in the same category as the Muslims and other Asians in the area. I found that my surname and marriage brought me more identification with the non-white community than with the white community. I certainly experienced, when out with my husband, the racism of the local white community, and probably more so than most. When we married in 1969 it was comparatively rare to have a mixed racial marriage, so I was very much looked down upon and despised.

The East End had been historically considered very racist, and as the white community saw the influx of immigrants moving into the area, they felt their existence was being threatened by foreign people bringing strange and different cultures to what they considered to be "their" land. This led to discrimination against people of other cultures.

In many cases racism became more overt and open. Feelings were not hidden, but expressed verbally and in violence. The difficulty for the Church was that the Asians in the area believed that all white British people were Christians, so what they were experiencing was directed at them by the Christian Church. In fact there was a certain amount of racism within the white Christian community and non-white people were often not welcomed into their churches. It was within this context that non-white people would be told by other churches in the area to go to St Andrew's Church because it was a 'black' church, even though the congregation at that time was only 30% non-white.

There was no glamour or status living in the East End. It was a place where people didn't want to come. Christians would go and work in the poorest of the Muslim countries but most wouldn't come to the East End of London. We were fortunate to always have a team of about six or more young university graduates helping us. This would often bring consternation from parents, who sometimes would ring and beg us not to take their son or daughter to work with us.

In the Old Testament, the stranger was a permanent reminder to the Jews of their past and how God rescued them from their wretched situation in a foreign land. This same God had called me to love those who were not loved, but who were despised and looked down upon. I had to identify with them as equals and in any other way I could. Coming from the friendly and open culture of New Zealand, I didn't find identification difficult as I always believed that I had to go to where people were, I couldn't expect them to come to me. I sat with the Muslim women where they sat and I listened to them. I prayed that daily I might have God's wisdom. If they needed any practical help I would try to assist, that I might show to them the love of Christ. Each was a person who was precious in God's eyes and of value. They were not a mass of poor people, but individuals, who needed to be served in all humility. Kenneth Leech who spent most of his life nearby to us in the East End of London, had found similar truths. He wrote "Poor people are our equals. They are not there as the objects of our care, not there in order to be "done good to". Christological caring is characterised by its ordinariness, by its humility, by its action rather than its words – feet washing is a silent ministry – and by its willingness to be contaminated by dirt and disease and blood".[3]

By ministering to people's practical needs we showed the love of Christ, and this was a sign of the Gospel, a non-verbal sharing of the Gospel of the Lord Jesus Christ. I find it very difficult to see a divide between the Gospel and social concern, as to my mind they are inextricably linked. Although during the 60s and 70s a divide developed in the Church between those who saw its mission as either evangelism or social action, we saw the Gospel as being social at its very heart.

Setting The Scene

Twice a year we visited every home within a one-mile radius of St Andrew's Centre. By doing this we were able to keep in touch with all the communities in the area. As a result, I have visited many Muslim homes over the years, and it is there that I have made friendships with Muslim women. I have studied the Bible with them, helped them fill in forms, gone on outings with them, taken them to hospital appointments and been with them in times of crisis. I have developed relationships with a number of these women over the years, and a close relationship with a few. I have tried to have a listening ear and in some cases have become a confidante. I have not attempted to sort out their problems, as a stranger can never do this; it has to be done within the family context. However I have been able to observe and discuss what happens behind the scenes in a Muslim home.

One subject that has been of interest to me has been the position and treatment of Muslim women in the home and in society at large. I saw that they had restrictions placed upon them, compared with their western counterparts. Some were not allowed out of the home unless accompanied by a male family member. The majority of Muslim women I met had to content themselves with looking after the home and the family, and that was their primary and only role. My visits would be whilst the husband was at work. If the husband believed I was visiting too frequently I would be asked (as happened in several cases) not to come again. He would be worried that I would impart western values to his wife, or lead her astray. Many Muslim women I found to be lonely and needing someone to talk to. The television and video would be on and that would be one of the main activities of her day.

Living in a foreign land often means that the extended family is not intact, as the majority of the family could still be in the country of origin. This can mean hardship for the wife, as she will have no-one to help her look after the children and will miss the companionship of other women members of the family.

It was out of this interest in Muslim women that I went to Westminster College in Oxford to study for a Masters Course. My subject was contextual change and Muslim women in Britain and Malaysia – can contextual change make a difference to the position of women? The subject enters the realm of social and religious change within the Muslim community. For the purpose of this book I have removed the sections on Malaysia, which were there to contrast and compare with the situation in the UK but were not major parts of the dissertation. The dissertation was submitted in September 1998. Since then I have updated and expanded various sections, removing the dialogue of each of the 30 interviews and where applicable adding it to the text of this book. I have also added to enrich this book my experience of many years in ministry to Muslim women.

The Structure Of The Interviews

Embarking on this project, I realised that I was entering the field of sensitive research where to obtain the true facts of the situation can be very difficult. Like many women, a Muslim woman will not want to divulge the facts about her life, or marriage, to a stranger, and Muslim young people, like most teenagers, will not want to divulge their innermost secrets except to their peers. The true facts can be masked. For example a wife might hide her difficulties from her husband and from the world, frightened that if she tells anyone her family might find out. The Muslim youth masks the facts from his family and the Muslim community.

I was recommended by the college to read Raymond Lee's book Doing Research on Sensitive Topics. He notes in his book that, "research poses an intrusive threat, dealing with areas which are private, stressful or sacred…information may be revealed which is stigmatising or incriminating….researchers often trespass into areas which are controversial or involve social conflict".[4] The researcher can be seen as one who wants discreditable information, as he seeks to find information about what is hidden, and about what people often wish to remain hidden. If it is revealed in the open it can stigmatise a community and become something which causes them to "lose face", to suffer the loss of their honor and dignity.

However in this current postmodern age, concealment is no longer acceptable, and there is virtually nothing left that is "sacred". It is an age where society demands transparency. However this tends not to be so with the non-western cultures within Britain, as they wish to show that all is well, that they have the answers for any ills and problems in their community and that they are coping with all its difficulties. They do not want their "dirty linen" to be aired in public. These societies wish to be seen as maintaining and upholding traditional values, and not as part of the western postmodern society with all its weaknesses and failures. It is very easy to understand and to be sympathetic with this idealistic position, but society has moved on, sweeping with it those from all cultures and backgrounds. An example of this age's interest in the details of other people's lives would be the success in the UK of novels such as Brick Lane, by Monica Ali. Like all novels it delves into the lives, backgrounds and personalities of its characters, not always in a positive light, and in this case the characters are Bengali Muslims living in London's East End. Some might consider it a sign of the integration of British culture that this novel was hugely popular. However there were strong objections to the book from within that community.

From a Christian point of view, we are called to love our neighbours and reach out to them, whoever they are. As part of this, it is good to understand something of people's beliefs and their circumstances, and the context in which they live, to help us understand and relate to them. The questions I asked about the difficulties women are facing were not made in a spirit of criticism but of seeking greater understanding for myself and others. As Christians, greater understanding can help lead us to greater love and prayer for those in difficult situations.

One of the most difficult things I had to face at the beginning of the research was how to obtain the information I required honestly and with integrity. I took the decision to do the research in the form of interviews by the non-directive, or 'depth' interviewing technique, where the interviewer takes a subordinate role. Lee advises that this is the preferential method for sensitive topics.[5] The interviews use long, open questions to ask questions about behaviour.[6] This gives the person being interviewed longer to think and to recall memory. Questions about sensitive topics are reached gradually through a series of less personal questions.[7]

Methodology

The interviews took place between November 1997 and July 1998. All the interviews were arranged for me by a local member of the Pakistani community, so very fortunately I was not coming into each situation from the cold. Individuals and families were chosen at random by another person who was in contact with many people within the Pakistani community. I was accompanied to each interview. The person introduced me and then either quietly left, or withdrew to another room and spoke with other members of the family. Some time prior to my arrival, permission had been sought for the interview and the reasons for it explained. It was all done completely in the open, with honesty and integrity.

All the interviews lasted approximately one and a half hours and, apart from those with young people, all took place in the interviewees' own homes. After the interview we had a cup of tea and the conversation continued. This part of the visit was very productive and each person really wanted to help as much as possible. I was conscious that what I wore, my attitudes and how I conducted myself made a difference.

With the young people I found it essential to interview them in a situation where no adult was present. I brought them to my home where they could feel relaxed and open to speak freely.

With several of the interviews the husband was present for all or part of the time. This was something I did not anticipate happening, and I had to be very careful and discreet in my approach. With an Ahmadiyya family the husband was present the whole time, apart from odd moments when he left the room. With another of the interviews the husband was present for the last third of the interview, but was absent for the tea and informal session at the end. I found that the presence of the husband in these two interviews was not positive. However in the seventh interview the husband was present from time to time and we were all able to have an open and frank conversation, both husband and wife discussing their marriage differences with me. This interview lasted much longer than all the other interviews, as they really felt the necessity to talk.

It was important that my approach was free of condemnation as I attempted to build up a relationship with the person I was interviewing. The first part of the interview was casual conversation about each other and just sharing who we were, the attitude was very informal. During the interview I realised very quickly that some of the conversations I was having were becoming very personal, so I ceased taking notes. I allowed the person just to go along the paths they wanted with just a prompting here and there. I had a series of issues I wanted to cover and I managed to obtain all the information I required with this approach. Much of the material obtained from the interview was written up at home directly afterwards.

The Choice Of Those To Be Interviewed

In the choice of those to be interviewed I wanted as large a spectrum as possible of different groups, ages, and social classes. Thus I covered both Sunni and Ahmadiyya Muslims, school and university students and women of various ages. I wanted to get a broad overview of what was happening. I also interviewed some Christian young people who had Muslim friends and could talk about their behaviour. Although I realise the limitations of talking to Christians about Muslims, they had seen and knew first hand about things that Muslim young people might not be in a position to admit to. One person I interviewed was a dinner lady in a college who did not consider herself staff and had no allegiance to them. She was a Muslim and had the ear of the Muslim girls, who would discuss their problems with her. I interviewed mothers with teenage children and those with younger children, and a woman who was a convert from Islam and runs a refuge for about thirty Muslim women. I interviewed the young who had been educated in the West and those from overseas, the uneducated, the middle class and the working class.

The Issues To Be Addressed

In the casual conversation at the beginning of the interview I attempted to find out particulars about each person: their age, whether they were married, where their husband worked, how many children they had and whether they were boys or girls and their ages, if their own marriage was arranged and whether they were going to arrange the marriages of their children. I asked them how long they had lived in Britain and whether they were educated here, and if they had gone out to work. These questions which can seem rude in a British context are perfectly acceptable in a Muslim context. However the questions go two ways; what I asked I also had to answer for myself.

There were certain issues to be covered in every interview, issues that I believe were the relevant ones to determine how contextualised the Muslim community was becoming to life in Britain. One of these was the issue of dating and marriage. Normally in a Muslim context there is no dating or mixing of the sexes after puberty and marriages are arranged. In Britain I was interested to know where their marriage partners would be found, in Britain or in their country of origin, whether the girls would be sent home to be married, and how frequently they returned to their country of origin.

Another issue was that of education and work. I wanted to find out how many girls were now going into further education, if they were going to a university away from home, and if they would work away from home. Would they work after they got married? How did the girls see marriage now that they were living in the West and what were their expectations of it? What about the children and the extended family network? Other questions were around the issues of marriage breakdown, the prevalence of divorce within the Muslim community, and the extremely sensitive area of violence within the home.

Then there were the issues of pre-marital sex, drugs, smoking, alcohol and dress. With the older women, I asked about whether living in Britain had changed their lives at all.

The Results Of The Survey

When I was conducting the interviews I found that people were very relaxed and willing to talk. The initial sharing time was very profitable and made people feel at ease. With the older women they were very willing to talk about their friends and what was happening and later on broadened it to cover their own situation. The conversation continued after the interview was finished and it was then they seem to be even more willing and open to talk. I was able to establish a good relationship with virtually everyone I interviewed, and they all wanted me to call again. I have visited many Muslim homes over the years so for me there was no threat or fear of anything new, as I felt completely at home in every situation.

This book begins with describing Islamic teaching and tradition about women. It then considers how particular aspects of teaching and tradition that concern women are applied in the lives of Muslim women in Britain today. In particular it looks to what degree their lives accommodate both their traditional faith and the western culture in which they now live.

Although I am obviously coming from the viewpoint of a Christian, and expect many readers to be Christians, I have not tried to compare Muslim history, teaching and traditions with those of the Christian Church. I have focused on trying to bring together the many different views of Muslim writers, from classical theologians to journalists in current magazines.

Women and Society

The Position of Women in pre-Islamic Arabia

In the sixth century after Christ the Arabs were a divided people broken into various tribes and at constant war with each other. There was no central government of any form in Arabia but unwritten laws which the tribes adhered to. However, the Jews and Christians had their scriptures but the Arabs were a people without a scripture, and ripe for a charismatic leader. There had not been the slightest hint of the Arabs feeling any urge to express their faith through an Arab medium.[1] Muhammad was to unite them and provide them with a purpose and an identity and a scripture. The result was power and triumph for a marginalised people who had been deeply divided and occupied in intertribal wars. Muhammad was to transform Arab society with regard to marriage and family relations with far-reaching consequences for women. These consequences were to remain unchanged throughout the centuries.

Marriage in Pre-Islamic Arabia

The marriage practices in the time before Islam were known as *Jahilial*. They were ones in which women enjoyed greater sexual freedom than was later allowed under Islam. This period of *Jahiliyyah* has been referred to as the "Age of Ignorance" or the "Age of Darkness" by Muslim society. They believe this was the time when people did not have the ability to distinguish between the permitted and the forbidden. Islam claims to have brought the criteria to them by which to distinguish between the licit and the illicit, and also to have clarified paternity. Muhammad saw his mission as bringing people from darkness into light.

There were many types of marriages at this time. These included polyandrous marriages (where the woman can have multiple husbands, the female equivalent of polygamy), which were also matrilineal marriages (where the family line descends through the mother). In this type of marriage the woman remains with her own tribe but entertains men as she pleases. Her husbands are from different tribes (except her own). When a child is born neither its actual father nor the tribe where it belongs can be determined with certainty, so the kinship descends down the female line. Another form of polyandry along with female kinship is when the unions are of a temporary nature and the wife dismisses her husbands at will.[2] Women who lived in a tent would dismiss their husband by turning the tent around. If it faced east they would turn it to face west and when the man saw this he knew he was dismissed and did not enter. If the tent belonged to a woman the man was received at her good pleasure.[3]

It is interesting to note that Muhammad's granddaughter, Sakina, married often and readily left the husbands she did not like. Women's independence from their husbands and their insistence on sexual self-determination seem to have been possible only because they were backed by their own people. This independence persisted even with the growing affirmation of patrilineal trends in the Arab society of Muhammad's time.[4]

Gertrude Stern in 1939 assessed marriage in this early community. Her work was a description of marriage processes, betrothal, consent, guardianship, dowry, adultery and the dissolution of marriage ties. She found no "fixed institution of marriage". She describes a diversity of sexual unions whose outstanding feature appears to be the looseness of marriage ties in general, and the lack of any legal system for regulating them.[5]

Islam Changes the Patterns of Marriage

Women's autonomy and participation were curtailed with the establishment of Islam, which also accelerated the transition from matriliny to patriliny. It did this by enforcing just one of the kinds of marriage common at the time, a marriage institution that had much in common with the patrilinial dominion marriage. It also condemned all matrilineal unions as *zina* (adultery).[6] In these new patriarchal kinship societies women were to have no will, no freedom, no independence and no opportunities of their own. They were treated as the chattels or possessions of their patriarchal kin group, in order to fulfil their basic biological function of procreation.[7] Social transformation had taken place.

Another kind of marriage permitted under Islam was *muta*, a marriage of pleasure or a temporary marriage. When a man would arrive in a new town on business or jihad, or when he was away from his family for extended periods, he could marry a woman in exchange for a sum of money. This amount would be according to the length of his stay. She would keep his belongings and take care of him. Its purpose was mutual living and sexual pleasure.[8]

Islam banished all practices in which the sexual self-determination of women was asserted. Muslim marriage gave absolute male authority a stamp of holy approval.[9]

Muhammad's Matrilineal Line

Muhammad's grandfather was the ruler of Mecca and the leader of the tribe of the Quraysh until he died.[10] He had ten sons his favourite being Abdullah. When the time came to find a marriage partner for Abdullah he looked for an alliance with another clan and sought the hand of Amina bint Wahb (Muhammad's mother) as a bride for his son. It was soon after this that Abdullah contracted a matrilineal marriage with Amina and later became Muhammad's father. As was the custom in matrilineal marriages, Amina remained with her own people. When they married, Abdullah stayed with Amina for only three days and then would visit her from time to time. This was the prevailing custom when the man decided to marry a woman who stayed with her own tribe.[11]

Abdullah died on a business trip to Medina when his wife was seven months pregnant. As a result Muhammad was the first and only child of the marriage. He left her very little: a slave, five camels and a few sheep.[12] A few years later Amina set out with Muhammad and her slave to visit the grave of her husband in Medina. On the way home she fell ill and died. Muhammad was then only six years old. His paternal grandfather then became his guardian and when he died, his uncle Abu Talib took over. The kinship had passed from the mother's to the father's line.[13]

Polygamy and Pre-Islamic Arabia

According to Muslim historians there were polygamous marriages before Muhammad where there was no restriction on the number of wives that a man could have. Tribal chiefs and leaders had many wives in order to build relationships with other families and make political alliances. It is reputed that there were instances of some men having from 10 to 500 wives.[14] As a result some argue that Muhammad improved the cultural position of the day by restricting the number of wives that a man could have to four.

This argument is disputed by Gertrude Stern and others. She has written that there is no reliable evidence of the practice of polygamy in pre-Islamic times at Medina or Mecca as understood in the Islamic era. She writes "from a study of the genealogical tables which I have compiled, there is no indication of a well-defined system of polygamy".[15] This is confirmed by Pickthall, whose translation of the Qur'an is well accepted. He states that Muhammad was concerned about the fate of women who were divorced, widowed or unmarried orphans, so he created a system of polygamy whereby unattached women were placed in a family unit in which a man would protect them, not just as kinsman but as husband. His suggestion that polygamy was instituted by the Qur'an after the disaster of Uhud, a battle in which many Muslim men were killed, substantiates this theory.[16]

Some do say however that contrary to the claims of Muslim historians, polygamy was not prevalent during the pre-Islamic period in Mecca and most certainly not in Medina. It was Muhammad who universalised and institutionalised multiple wife-taking, mainly to justify his own practice when he fled his home town and after he assumed power in Medina. According to Hekmat, Muhammad may have repressed his sexual passions, not daring to bring them out in the open, while his powerful wife was alive. But from the description he gives of paradise in the Qur'an one can safely assume that the idea of enjoying the companionship of young beautiful women was an inate quality and always part of him as long as he lived.[17]

Common Practices in Pre-Islamic Arabia

When a girl was born in pre-Islamic Arabia, it brought great shame and disgrace. The practice of infanticide existed in Arabia at this time. Some say that this had pride as the motive, as parents were afraid that if their daughters were taken captive they might bring disgrace on their tribe. Others say that the motive was poverty. However evidence appears to show that these two motives belonged to distinct varieties of this practice.[18] In Arabia female infanticide was carried out in such a way so that no blood was shed: the infant was buried alive or the grave ready by the side of the bed on which the daughter was born.[19] This practice was concerned with fears of female frailty, and even in the most civilised period of the Caliphate we find the death of a daughter in childhood regarded as a subject for congratulation, the father being thereby saved from a possible source of danger to his honor. An older theory is that a man is disgraced by giving his flesh and blood into another man's power. Where infanticide was not practised fear of dishonor led to child marriage.[20]

The Qur'an spoke out against the practice of female infanticide, and in later verses forbade it. Muhammad went further and said that it was unacceptable for parents to discriminate unfairly in favour of their sons.

The Qur'an is also credited with removing the uncertainties around women's inheritance by fixing a share in inheritance for women, even though it was half that of a similar male blood relative. This had the effect of a bombshell on the male population of Medina, who found themselves for the first time in direct personal conflict with the Muslim God. Before this, men were assured of their rights of inheritance in Arabia, and women were part of the inherited goods. When a man died his eldest son inherited his widow. He could, if she was not his own mother, either marry her or pass his rights over her to his brother or his nephew, if he so desired. They could then marry her in his place. As far as the men were concerned the new regulations on inheritance tampered with matters in which Islam should not intervene – their relations with women.[21]

These two edicts are the basis of the argument that Islam improved the position of women.

Muhammad and his Wife Khadija

Muhammad seems to have remained a bachelor longer than most, probably because of his poverty. It is interesting to look at his first wife, Khadija Bint Khuwaylid, who also belonged to the tribe of Quraysh, a tribe whose ancestry they claim goes back to Ishmael. She was forty and Muhammad twenty-five when they married. It was the *Jahiliyyah* customs of the day that shaped her conduct and position in life rather than Islamic – for example, her economic independence, her freedom, her marriage to a man many years younger than herself, and her monogamous marriages. She was typical of members of the Quraysh aristocracy, full of initiative in public life as well as private life.[22]

Khadija's fortune was one of the greatest in Mecca. She had been married twice to Makhumite bankers, and had a child by each. With the help of her father, Khowailid, her commercial business which she directed, had become one of the most important in this "Venice of the desert".[23] She was very wealthy and powerful and had built up and ran a flourishing business of importing spices and silks which were sent by caravan to Syria and Palestine. She employed Muhammad, and later proposed to him. She "asked for the hand of the Prophet", because she said she found in him the qualities she most appreciated in a man.[24] It was most likely because of her wealth and status that she could insist that he would remain monogamous during her lifetime, or it was most likely written in the marriage contract. She supported him with an allowance for the duration of her life and gave him a slave who later became his adopted son. Khadija was convinced that he was no ordinary husband and she had complete confidence in him.

Muhammad may have realised that marriage to the wealthy widow who was blessed with the fortunes of two husbands could provide him with enough means to pursue his social goals. He was well aware that no political or social achievement is reached without enough social backing.[25] It was her wealth that allowed Muhammad to be free to contemplate and later to go around preaching. However Khadija retained the management of her wealth, supplying Muhammad with whatever he needed. She died at the age of sixty-five, and within days Muhammad had married again. His new wife was also a widow. She was called Sauda. In the subsequent marriages of Muhammad after Khadija, autonomy for women and monogamy were no longer a characteristic.

Muhammad and his Wife Aisha

Muhammad's third and favourite wife, Aisha, married him when she was six years old and was the daughter of his close friend and early convert, Abu Bakr. The marriage was consummated when she was nine and still playing with her dolls. In this period of time and in places where female infanticide was not practiced, the fear of dishonor led to child marriage, with seven or eight being the normal age at which girls became wives.[26]

Aisha along with her co-wives began to observe the new customs of veiling and seclusion which foreshadowed the changes that Islam would effect upon Arabian women. It could have been Muhammad's suspicion of Aisha's unfaithfulness that led to the changes for women within Islam. After Muhammad's death Aisha briefly assumed political leadership with the authority of the community. She had lived in a time of transition and her life reflected both *Jahilial* and Islamic practice. Women having authority over the affairs of the community began declining with the advent of Islam.

The Position of Women before Islam

We see that the status of women during the pre-Islamic period was not necessarily as bad as has been suggested by later Muslim historians. Wealthy women of a higher status were held in high esteem and certain customs and rules did not apply to them.[27] There were women who ignored their father's decision and chose their own marriage partners. These women, like Khadija, lived independent lives and were free to make their own decisions and could even divorce. However their independence and sometimes political power was derived from their financial status. Hand in hand with some women achieving respected and powerful positions was also the total subjugation of women and the practice of female infanticide.

In the ensuing Islamic period the situation was different. Mohammad Arafa in his book "The Rights of Women in Islam" maintains that in the whole history of Islam there is no mention of the participation of women alongside men in the direction of the affairs of state, whether in political decision making or in strategic planning.[28] The great exception to this was Aisha.

The powerful Aisha

Aisha was Muhammad's favourite wife who was only eighteen when he died. Muhammad died on Monday June 8th in 632 AD and his body was left in the corner of Aisha's room. Everyone was so caught up in the election of the successor that nobody thought of washing the body or burial, and he was not buried until the Wednesday night. The struggle for political power in Islam had begun.[29]

At the age of forty-two Aisha took to the battlefield at the head of an army against the ruling caliph Ali. Ali had been chosen as caliph in Medina in 656 AD, causing many Muslims to take up arms, as they challenged his legitimacy. Aisha had reproached Ali for not having brought the murderers of the assassinated third caliph to justice. She took command of the army and fought Ali at Basra. Aisha had gone against the rule instituted by Muhammad in the

Hadith that says a woman cannot take part in fighting. She is able to go to the battlefield however, to treat the wounded and to give water, as well as cooking and feeding those taking part in *jihad*. Ali requested his army to shoot at the camel and not Aisha. When the camel was dead her voice was then lost in the noise of battle as she could no longer command her army from the position of power. Ali inflicted a crushing defeat on her.

The historians called this confrontation "The Battle of the Camel", referring to the camel ridden by Aisha and thereby avoiding linking in the memory of Muslim girls the name of a woman with the name of a battle.[30] It was after this battle, according to Sahih al-Bukhari (a collection of Hadith, or sayings of Muhammad), that it was reported that Abu Bakra had heard the Prophet say "Those who entrust their affairs to a woman will never know prosperity". This Hadith is recognised as being an authentic Hadith by being included in the Sahih.[31] (Sahih before the collector's name means "true", i.e. a particularly reliable and authentic collection)

It is reputed that 15,000 people were killed in a few hours in the Battle of the Camel. Ali, weakened by this battle, had then to confront another political adversary Mu'awiya the Governor of Syria. They met at the Battle of Siffin which was long and bloody with 70,000 men dead. In the end arbitration took place and Mu'awiya was designated as Caliph. This resulted in the split between the Sunnis and Shi'ites.

Al Afghani, the first modern Islamic reformer of the 19th Century, is convinced that Aisha was not only responsible for the blood spilt at the Battle of the Camel which set in motion the split of the Muslim world into two factions (Sunnis and Shi'ites), but she was also responsible for all the subsequent losses for those that followed. He claims that if Aisha had not intervened in the public affairs of the Muslim state, "Muslim history would have taken the path of peace, progress and prosperity". According to him, Allah wanted to use the experience of Aisha to teach the Muslims a lesson. "Allah created women to reproduce the race, bring up future generations, and be in charge of households. He wanted to teach Muslims a practical lesson that they cannot forget".[32]

What Islam Says About Women

For the Muslim, the Qur'an is the eternal word of God, his final revelation which was given to the Muslim prophet Muhammad. It is the holy book of the Muslims and they believe it is the final source of authority. It is considered to be the source not only of true religion but also of knowledge. Muslims believe that the Qur'an in Arabic is the exact replica of tablets preserved in heaven which was with God from the very beginning. Therefore they say that the Qur'an was "uncreated" and eternal. They believe that it was revealed to Muhammad over a period of twenty three years by the angel Gabriel word perfect from the tablets in heaven.

Within the Qur'an itself are seemingly contradictory statements, but according to the "doctrine of abrogation" the later verses or suras supersede the earlier ones where there are inconsistencies.

Islamic teaching comes not only from the Qur'an but also from the Hadith. The collection of Hadith or traditions, record the words and deeds of Muhammad. It must be noted that the words of the Hadith are not always the words of Muhammad but how the people known as the "Companions of the Prophet" understood them, or what people were saying or doing at that time. It is necessary to check the identity of the "Companion of the Prophet" who uttered it and in what circumstances, as well as the chain of people who passed it along. There is also the difficulty of the authenticity of the tradition, whether it is weak, forged or authentic.

When the Qur'an and traditions are silent on a particular subject, rules are derived by consensus of the religious leaders (*ijma*) and by analogous reasoning (*qiyas*). The combination of Qur'an, Hadith, *ijma* and *qiyas* have been used by Islamic scholars to create the body of rules and regulations known as the *Shari'a* or Islamic Law.

What is Equality?

Equality is the acceptance of the dignity of the sexes in equal measure, including equal rights for both men and women covering social, economic, political and legal areas. Both should have the equal right to contract a marriage or dissolve it, to buy or dispose of property, and to choose their own profession. Men and women should be equal in responsibility as well as in freedom. Fundamental to Christianity is the equal worth of men and women in the sight of God.

What Islam says about the Equality of Women

Muslims believe that the Qur'an without any doubt teaches the equality of men and women. They say that there was never any dispute about this: men and women are equal. The suras or verses of the Qur'an that they quote are the following[1] :

> *O mankind, be careful of your duty to your Lord. Who created you from a single soul and from it created its mate and from them twain hath spread abroad a multitude of men and women.*[2]

Islam holds that this verse shows that one is not superior over the other, as both men and women have originated from one being, and therefore enjoy equal status.

> *O mankind! Lo! We have created you from a male and a female.*[3]

Islam believes this verse means men and women are equal.

We have honored the children of Adam.[4]

Muslims say that "children of Adam" means that both men and women are equally honored without any distinction of sex.

By these three verses Muslims claim there is no doubt that the Qur'an teaches that men and women are equal. However this theoretical equality has not been seen in practice. Some Muslim scholars have recognised this and say that these verses affirming equality have not been followed, and that it is essential to hold a thorough enquiry into the plight of women. The many rights that have been given to women by Islam and have in practice been ignored should be restored to them.[5]

Equality is also explained by another argument, that men and women are equal but they have different functions related to biology. That while men are the physically stronger sex, the women's biological make-up has made her excel as a homemaker.[6] This is saying that a woman's role is restricted because of her biology and so she is only capable of doing domestic work. In the UK, years of struggle for women's rights and two world wars have laid this discriminatory argument to rest, but even echoes of it are still seen from time to time.

Within Islam, this view is vigorously contested by women like Wadud-Muhsin who argue against the values that have been attributed to women as weak, inferior, inherently evil, intellectually incapable and spiritually lacking, making them unsuitable for performing certain tasks or functioning in different ways in society. They have in fact been restricted to functions related to their biology.[7] She feels that a woman's role is greatly limited because of pre-conceptions of what her role should be. These values attached to being a woman are degrading, humiliating and give her a lower position in society.

The Religious Status of Women in Islam

The Qur'an says:

> *Lo men who surrender unto Allah, and women who surrender, and men who believe and women who believe, and men who obey and women who obey, and men who speak the truth and women who speak the truth, and men who persevere (in righteousness) and women who persevere, and men who are humble and women who are humble, and men who give alms and women who give alms, and men who fast and women who fast, and men who guard their modesty and women who guard (their modesty) and men who remember Allah much and women who remember - Allah has prepared for them forgiveness and a vast reward.*[8]

Muslims point out that this verse addresses women directly ten times, which proves that women can attain the same as men and settles it conclusively that in the Qur'an women stand on the same spiritual level. This passage "makes a clear statement about the absolute identity of the human moral condition and identical spiritual and moral obligations placed on all individuals regardless of sex."[9]

The presence of verses such as these in the Qur'an "explains why Muslim women frequently insist, often inexplicably to non-Muslims, that Islam is not sexist. They hear and read in its sacred text, justly and legitimately, a different message from that heard by the makers and enforcers of orthodox, androcentric Islam."[10]

However it is easy to look at only certain verses in the Qur'an and come to the position that the Qur'an teaches that men and women are equal both in position and religious status. Many Muslims believe that the Qur'an does teach equality, even though they admit that equality does not exist in the real world. However before we come to a conclusion we need to look at other verses in the Qur'an and Hadith and weigh up the evidence in totality.

The Woman's Destination in Eternity

In the Hadith it says:

Once Allah's Apostle said to a group of women, "O women! Give alms, as I have seen that the majority of the dwellers of Hell-fire were you (women)." They asked, "Why is it so, O Allah's Apostle?" He replied, "You curse frequently and are ungrateful to your husbands. I have not seen anyone more deficient in intelligence and religion than you. A cautious sensible man could be led astray by some of you." The women asked, "O Allah's Apostle! What is deficient in our intelligence and religion?" He said, "Is not the evidence of two women equal to the witness of one man?" They replied in the affirmative. He said, "This is the deficiency in your intelligence. Isn't it true that a woman can neither pray nor fast during her menses?" The women replied in the affirmative. He said, "This is the deficiency in her religion".[11]

This Hadith is considered to be genuine and authentic and is reported by both Al Bukhari and Muslim, two of the most reliable collections of Hadith. It is undisputed and used by eminent scholars.

And again another Hadith reads:

The Prophet said "I looked into Paradise and found that the majority of its dwellers were the poor people, and I looked into (Hell) fire and found that the majority of its dwellers were women".[12]

There are seven other references by Al-Bukhari in the Hadith about hell being full of women.[13] These are very credible sayings because of the source and reinforced by the number of times they appear.

The question is how does a woman get into paradise? The wife has to be absolutely obedient to her husband which shows her piety and guarantees her eternal destiny. If she gives him trouble and anxiety she will not be able to be his wife in paradise. Then the pure-eyed virgin girls (*houris*) will be his consorts. He is her paradise or her hell. The husband is so elevated that by comparison with the woman he is placed on a divine level. Her response to him has to approach worship of him.[14] This is seen in the following Hadith when Muhammad said,

> *"If I were to command anyone to prostation before another, I would command women to prostate themselves before their husbands, because of the special right over them given to husbands by Allah".*[15]

The wives of the righteous and obedient are mentioned as accompanying their husbands in paradise. Women in paradise must be submissive, subordinate, veiled and secluded in the harems of heaven, watching quietly as their husbands make love with the beautiful *houris* of paradise. Man is her master on earth, and she will be subjugated to him forever in heaven as well. In the whole text of the Qur'an there is not one verse to show that women will be treated equally in paradise. The sexuality of the man is recognised, sanctioned and amply provided for by the Muslim scripture, but the needs of women are totally left out. Some descriptions of paradise mention "immortal youths" who serve wine to husbands, there is no implication that women are given the same sexual freedom with these youths as the men are allowed with the *houris*. Women in paradise must be faithful to their husbands as they were in their earthly existence.[16]

In the Qur'an it says:

> *They and their wives, in pleasant shade, on thrones reclining.*[17]

Why Women go to Hell

It says in the Hadith,

> *"I also saw the Hell-fire and I had never seen such a horrible sight. I saw that most of the inhabitants were women." The people asked, "O Allah's Apostle! Why is it so?" The Prophet replied, "Because of their ungratefulness." He was asked whether they were ungrateful to Allah.*

The Prophet said, "They are ungrateful to their companions of life (husbands) and ungrateful to good deeds".[18]

If we look at all the verses about eternal destiny the evidence appears to suggest that unless a woman is obedient and grateful to her husband at the time of death she will go to hell. All her piety will be considered useless if she disobeys him. However if she is obedient she will then be with him in heaven. It is interesting to note that nothing is said about women martyrs being in heaven, or about single women.

Women Considered Deficient in Intelligence

The Hadith quoted at the start of the section above states that women are deficient in intelligence, as well as in religion. One Muslim male feminist writer reasons that if men are superior to women in physical strength and intelligence, it is because men were engaged in work activities that required them to use their brains and bodies and therefore to develop them. Women have been deprived of all opportunity and forced into an inferior position.[19]

It does seem to be a well established view that has lasted over the centuries that women are not as intelligent as men.

Women lack Gratitude

This is expressed in the Hadith from Bukhari

Women are ungrateful to their husbands and are ungrateful for the favours and the good (charitable) deeds done to them. If you have always been good (benevolent) to one of them and then she sees something in you (not of her liking), she will say, "I have never received any good from you".[20]

This deficiency of the woman in intelligence, religion and gratitude prevents her from exchanging secular or sacred ideas or participating in religious or related activities.

Men's Superiority

The Qur'an says:

Men are in charge of women, because Allah has made the one of them to excel the other.[21]

or as Dawood's translation reads:

Men have authority over women because Allah has made the one superior to the others.[22]

We see the Qur'an stating very clearly here that the men are superior to women because they have been given authority over them.

Muslim theologians appear to have held with the social prejudices of the day regarding women to be inferior to men and even showing contempt for them. This is seen in a considerable amount in the Hadith literature, where women are described as a source of evil and lust who lead men to hell. Social prejudices seem to have played an important part in the personal narrations. Traditions that were passed on from one narrator to another over a large span of time were affected by the distortions of social prejudice as well as the distortions of memory.

Some Muslim women believe that the position of women in the Qur'an is misinterpreted by the prejudice of men. Wadud-Muhsin says that most Muslim men have at one time or another heard, or perhaps even believed, that women are "inferior" and "unequal" to men. The prejudices and attitudes amongst Muslim men have not only affected the position of women in Muslim societies but also affected the interpretation of the position of women in the Qur'an.[23]

An example of a writer who demonstrates such prejudices is Nadvi, who says that no sensible person can deny the fact that the man, due to his innate capabilities, is superior to woman in many ways. He claims that present day knowledge also supports the view of the superiority of men in that it has been found that a man's brain is much larger in volume than that of a woman, which he believes shows that he is superior to her in intellect and also in maturity.[24]

Women are 'Aura (nakedness)

The Encyclopedia of Islam defines the word *aura* as the external genitals or it could mean defect, weak spot or blemish. In the Islamic text it means the part of the body which needs to be covered. In an authentic Hadith, Muhammad said,

> *The woman is "aura". When she goes outside (the house) the devil welcomes her.*

All the female body is taken to be aura (i.e. the nakedness of her husband or male family member) *Ibn Taymiyya* even argued that a fingernail of a woman is aura. This Hadith has been used to convince millions of women all over the world to cover up. Another Hadith states,

> *Women have ten "aurat". When she gets married her husband covers one, and when she dies the grave covers the ten.*

The female body is considered desirable, therefore when a female leaves the home she becomes defenseless and vulnerable to the eyes of men. This reduces men's piety and makes them susceptible to seduction. Another Hadith asserts that when a man sees a woman approaching, she comes in the form of Satan.

These are signs of male superiority and control.

Discipline of Women

The Qur'an says:

> *So good women are the obedient, guarding in secret that which Allah hath guarded. As for those from whom you fear rebellion, admonish*

them and banish them to beds apart, and scourge them. Then if they obey you, seek not a way against them.[25]

The above verse was revealed in connection with a woman who complained to Muhammad that her husband slapped her on the face (which was still marked with the slap). At first Muhammad told her to get even with him, and then added. "Wait until I think about it". Later on the above sura was revealed, after which the Muslim prophet said

"We wanted one thing but Allah wanted another, and what Allah wanted is best."[26]

This verse permits wife beating. The man has the responsibility to admonish his wife, the right to desert her sexually by moving into separate beds, and to beat her to correct any rebelliousness in behaviour. The sexual desertion is a remedy to curb the rebelliousness of the woman and to humiliate her pride. The word "rebellion" here refers to any disobedience on the part of the woman, not simply a refusal to engage in sex. If she refuses to sleep with her husband or does not obey his command, she will be admonished first, and later the man is permitted by Allah to beat his wife.

The wife of a Muslim should always be ready to come to bed and satisfy her husband's sensual desires, otherwise she may be beaten by him and cursed by the angels of Allah, who are commissioned to have a close watch over the sexual affairs of a couple.[27] Muhammad is quoted as saying,

"If a man invites his wife to sleep with him and she refuses to come to him, then the angels send their curses on her until morning."[28]

A man's sexual desires are considered so urgent that it is better to let food burn in the oven than let his desires remain unfulfilled.

When a man calls his wife to satisfy his desire she must go to him even if she is occupied at the oven.[29]

And again

> *When a man calls his wife to his bed, and she refuses, the One who is in heaven will be angry with her until he (her husband) is pleased with her.*[30]

Wife beating was very common in Muhammad's, time, and some Muslims claim that this reflected the sociological conditions of the day. Some scholars say that the verse should be interpreted differently in today's context. Because the verse was revealed in a certain sociological context they claim it must be seen as such, and not as normative for all times to come. The difficulty with this is that Muslim jurists see this verse as normative and not able to be changed. What we see in practice is that wife beating is considered to be sanctioned in the Qur'an. As one Muslim scholar puts it "There is wickedness and weakness in women. Diplomacy and harshness is the remedy for wickedness and gentleness is the remedy for weakness." [31]

Women Deficient as Witnesses

In the Qur'an it says:

> *And call to witness, from among your men, two witnesses. And if two men be not (at hand) then a man and two women, of such as ye approve as witnesses, so that if the one erreth (through forgetfulness) the other will remember.*[32]

From this Muslim jurists have firmly asserted that it is divine intervention that one male witness is equal to two women witnesses. They also assert that the witness given by two women will be valid only when accompanied by a man. If two male witnesses are not available then there should be one man and two women, not four women. Four women cannot replace two men.

This is repeated in a verse in the Hadith: Allah's Apostle said to a group of women,

> *"Is not the evidence of two women equal to the witness of one man?" They replied in the affirmative. He said, "This is the deficiency in your intelligence."* [33]

Women and Inheritance

In the Qur'an it says:

> *Allah chargeth you concerning (the provision for) your children: to the male the equivalent of the portion of two females.* [34]

We have women being given half the share of the male heirs.

The modernists argue that this verse does injustice to a daughter as she has been given half that of a son and the basis of this is bias against the female sex. A more common view is that it was a cautious reform in favour of daughters, as in pre-Islamic society daughters did not inherit at all and now they were given the right to inherit half that of a son. [35] This is an area where Islam claims to have improved the position of women.

The Veil

In the Qur'an it says:

> *And tell the believing women to lower their gaze and be modest and to display of their ornament only that which is apparent, and to draw their veils over their bosoms.* [36]

There are varying views as to what ornament or adornment means. Tabari says that it means the clothes that a woman wears, and the injunction to draw their veils over their bosoms was in response to the uncovered breasts of tribal women. There is no injunction in the Qur'an that she should veil her face or head, though it was the cultural practice of some societies of the day such as the upper classes of the Byzantine Christians. It was claimed that this verse was to save women from being objects of lust, and that it was to elevate women above their sexuality.

Some attribute the veil to Umar, Muhammad's father-in-law and close friend. Umar told Muhammad that it is proper to order his wives to wear veils because some men who enter his house may have wicked minds. Another story is that Aisha went to visit Muhammad wearing a flimsy dress. He said to her that when a woman reaches puberty, it is not appropriate for any part of her body to be seen except "this and this." He pointed to his face and hands.[37]

Purdah has been a Muslim institution for about a thousand years and was gradually established during the first three centuries of Islam. It was fully established by the tenth and eleventh centuries and is now an integral part of Muslim life. The Purdah system is an extreme form of male dominance as it denies women the freedom of action and participation in social life.

In his attempt to grasp the logic of the seclusion and veiling of women and the basis of sexual segregation, the Muslim feminist Qasim Amin came to the conclusion that women are better able to control their sexual impulses than men and that consequently sexual segregation is a device to protect men rather than women. He asks who fears what in such societies. Observing that women do not appreciate seclusion very much and conform to it only because they are compelled to, he concluded what is feared is the "femme fatale" who causes disorder and chaos.[38]

He then asked, "Who is protected by seclusion?" If what men fear is that women might succumb to their masculine attraction, why did they not institute veils for themselves? Are men considered less able than women to control themselves and resist their sexual impulses? He concludes that preventing women from showing themselves unveiled expresses men's fear of losing control over their minds, and thus being tempted by any woman they see.[39]

The Characteristics of Islamic Marriage

Like a contract of sale, an Islamic marriage involves an exchange of goods and services. In exchange for dowry *mahr* and daily maintenance *nafaqih* which the wife receives, the husband gains exclusive ownership right *tamlik* over his wife's sexuality and reproductive activities and, by extension over her person. According to Islamic law, the woman is to give her consent, however nominally, and it is the woman not her father who receives the full amount of dowry (custom aside).

The dowry is a technical term denoting the money or goods which must be given to the woman in the marriage contract. We see this rooted in the Qur'an:

> *Give them their dowry for the enjoyment you have had of them as a duty.*[40]

However the moment a woman agrees to a marriage contract, she is understood to have relinquished voluntarily all control and autonomy she may have had over her own legal and social rights. After the conclusion of the contract she is legally and conceptually associated with the object of exchange and comes under the legal authority of her husband. Within the structure of the marriage contract a woman's sexual and reproductive activity is at the core of the economic and social transaction. A woman's sexuality is identified with her whole being.[41]

Men view women as objects to be owned and jealously controlled; as objects of desire to seclude, to veil and to discard; and at the same time objects of indispensable value to men's sense of power and virility. This contract dictates a wife's obedience to her husband, while limiting her autonomy. The obedience to her husband and to the larger social order is reciprocated with financial security in the family and prestige in society.[42]

Polygamy and the Qur'an

The Qur'an says:

> *If you fear that you cannot treat orphans with fairness, then you may marry other women who seem good to you, two or three or four of them. But if you fear that you cannot maintain equality among them, marry only one.*[43]

It has been argued that polygamy was necessary to establish social justice by allowing men to marry orphans and widows. Some, however, have argued that maintaining equality between wives is impossible, so marrying more than one wife is not permissible. They point out that even Muhammad loved his wife Aisha more than any of the others when he practiced polygamy.

Again in the Qur'an:

> *Try as you may you cannot treat all of your wives impartially. Do not set yourself altogether against any of them.*[44]

Polygamy is a discriminatory decree against women to the benefit of men in Muslim society. This is a one sided privilege, given solely to men, which leads to the segregation of women from men, resulting in women being gradually driven out of most socioeconomic activities, as is largely the case in the Muslim world today. The results of polygamy are conspiracies, quarrels and jealousies amongst the different wives, and sometimes beating, death threats, even poisoning and killing of children. Moreover women under these conditions are humiliated and are looked upon as slave girls or even as a commodity.[45]

Divorce and the Qur'an

Divorce can happen very easily in Islam. The power of divorce resides in the hand of the man. In the Qur'an it says:

And if ye wish to exchange one wife for another...[46]

This verse gives the man absolute power to repudiate his wife and to marry someone else. There are no formalities. According to the *Shari'a* a man has only to repeat "I divorce you" three times in front of witnesses and the wife is thrown out of the house. There is no court, judge, lawyer or counsellor. The woman who is divorced may not remarry for at least three months as she must observe a waiting period of three menstrual cycles. At the end of the three months the divorce is irrevocable. During this three month period the husband can revoke the divorce just by taking his wife back to live with him. By returning she has the status of a wife again.

For a woman it is very difficult to divorce her husband and in most cases is futile. However she can sue on the grounds of impotency of the husband, non-payment of maintenance or his insanity. Cruelty is not sufficient grounds for divorce, as wife beating is an injunction of the Qur'an. After the marriage is dissolved and finalised the husband is supposed to provide for his former wife's subsistence. He need only do this for three months.

Custody of the Children

When a man divorces the children are considered to be the property of the husband. Being a Muslim does not give the right to custody of the children.

However, the mother can have rights to look after a son up to the age of seven, as long as he is safe from apostasy or corruption. If she is seen taking the child to church or feeding him pork the father has the right to take the child. The mother may have custody of a daughter up to the age of puberty which is considered to be nine years old. If she rejects Islam she cannot have custody of the children. If she remarries she loses custody of the children unless the new husband is related to the child as a paternal uncle.

Conclusion

Islam claims to believe in the equality of the sexes but having looked at the verses about women quoted in the Qur'an and the quotations from the Hadith there is not consistency. The man is said to be superior in many ways. Women are considered deficient in intelligence, gratitude, and religion, permitted to be beaten, can be one of several wives, and no real possibility of attaining heaven. They also do not have equal rights in regard to divorce, being a witness, inheritance and custody of the children. These laws are all weighted in favour of the man. In fact we can come to the conclusion that the sources of Islam do not guarantee equal human rights for women.

Muslims claim that it is important to take into account the sociological influences in interpreting scripture, as no reading or rendering of a text can be free of such influences. The interpretations must be seen within the sociological perspective of the time where women were seen as mere chattels, producing children and providing pleasure for the husband. Thus the men who formulated *Shari'a,* or Islamic law, over a period of two centuries or more were influenced in their interpretation of the Qur'an and Hadith by the misogynist environment in which they lived. The problem is that the sociological became the theological and has been defended as such, even when sociological conditions have changed.

The sociological argument has its strengths and weaknesses. Muhammad must have been influenced by the sociological conditions of the day and the words attributed to him will reflect that, as will the interpretations of the early theologians and jurists involved in creating the body of rules that is Islamic law. But that remains in tension with verses from the Qur'an that sanction a discriminatory view of women. The classical view of Islam regards the Qur'an as a direct revelation from Allah to Muhammad, perfectly preserved in oral form from the beginning, and therefore not able to be affected by sociological conditions.

Muslim reformers since the 18th century have insisted that Islam is capable of coming to terms with modernity. In particular they have claimed that the *Shari'a* has enshrined in its various schools certain principles of development which allow jurists to extend or to limit the application of law and to formulate it in fresh ways appropriate to changing circumstances. In many countries such *ijtihad* or independent judgement has led to significant changes in family law. This has happened in places like Tunisia, and Morocco.

However many others consider the *Shari'a* to be totally divine and immutable. They believe the gates of *ijtihad* were closed in the 11th century. That meant that the law was now fixed and was unable to be changed to suit varying situations. In countries or situations where *Shari'a* is considered to be fixed and is imposed on the population, the position and rights of women is the same as it was many centuries ago. In some countries the civil law runs alongside the *Shari'a* law and women in these countries have more rights on issues such as divorce. However there is a mood for many countries to return to an unreformed Islam, that is a strict Shari'a. Whenever this takes place the position of women and their rights take a backward step.

Understanding the
Concept of Honor and Shame

In the West, society has been underpinned by the Judeo-Christian ethic which gives clear guidelines on what is right and wrong. This "right versus wrong" perspective dictates much of our thinking. We teach our children to act in a right manner and if they don't we teach them feelings of guilt as the proper response. However the Muslim world does not operate on this paradigm and the right versus wrong perspective does not have the same power and influence. The society dictates what is acceptable and unacceptable, right and wrong rarely become a factor.[1]

The importance of Family Honor

There are three fundamentals of Muslim society, honor, shame and revenge. The family's honor or *izzat* is maintained by conforming to the social norms of the society and by the absence of any visible shame. Islam means "submission" or to conform. The very object of the pillars or duties of Islam such as prayers and fasting are to enforce conformity on all its followers. Conformity is valued as it brings honor and social prestige to the family. Individualism as we have in the West is criticised as Muslims believe it does not benefit the family and the lack of conformity can lead to shame from the community. There is an old Arab saying that "innovation is the root of all evil". The individual is not important in Islam, it is the family and community that matters.

Muslim children are taught to act honorably, and if they fail, feelings of shame are the proper response. Children are readily told by any member of the family if they are doing something shameful. This is to enable them to learn the boundaries of personal behaviour. Shame can be caused by not looking after your family, by losing your temper and shouting insults at a person, by harmful gossip or even failure, amongst other things. Cases of failure, unless the blame can be apportioned to another person, suicide can be seen as the honorable way out.

Honor is shown in many ways, by hospitality where both the family and the guest are honored or by agreeing with a member of the family (even if you don't agree with them), bestows honor on them. This paradigm penetrates all aspects of society and life, to what chair you sit on, who goes through the door first, by the giving of gifts and by generally doing good deeds to others. Honor is achieved by passing exams, by marriage, by giving birth to a boy. You can never confer honor on yourself, it comes from others by what they see or perceive to see. Age brings honor; there is a saying "He who is one day older than you is wiser by one year." Honor is placed on a family, or on a tribe or even on a nation. A whole nation can be honored, or shamed and "lose face" in the sight of the world.

Shame and the Effects on the Family

If a member of the family is responsible for any wrongdoing or if they are in circumstances that could be conceived as shameful, it has to be kept within the family circle and hidden from the outside world. This must be done at all costs otherwise the family will be shamed. Even the birth of a baby girl can be considered shameful and the birth goes unannounced. Condolences can be given to the father. So honor and shame become the controlling forces in people's lives.

Shame is not only an act against the accepted system of values but it can also include the discovery by outsiders that the act has been committed. A person who has done a shameful act must conceal it, for revealing the disgrace is to commit another disgrace. There is an Arab proverb that says "a concealed shame is two thirds forgiven". To avoid this shame, lying or concealment is seen as honorable and therefore the right thing to do. However if a shameful act cannot be covered up by any means it must be avenged. This is sanctioned by the Qur'an:

Believers, retaliation is decreed for you in bloodshed. [2]

Here we enter the realm of honor killings which we will deal with later. Following the same principle, if a tribe feels it has been shamed, tribal warfare can result. I met a young Muslim girl who at the age of five had been betrothed to a boy in Pakistan. She is now eighteen and does not want to marry this boy, but wishes to choose her own marriage partner from Britain. This is causing great worry for her parents who are now questioning their judgement in carrying out this "act of betrothal". The parents are caught in a dilemma. If she does not go ahead with the marriage the family will be shamed, if she does she will be forced into a marriage she doesn't want. They are caught in an impossible situation, which is causing them great distress.

The Division of Honor and Shame

While in theory codes of honor and shame refer to the behaviour of both men and women, in practice honor is generally seen as men's responsibility and shame as women's. The division of honor and shame is related to the fact that honor is seen as actively achieved whilst shame is seen as passively defended, resulting in different expectations of men and women. Inherent in this notion of female shame is the concept of female sexuality which requires social control.[3]

The underlying issue in the definition of shame is the sexual control of women in particular, and the younger generation in general. If a woman refuses an arranged marriage, has an affair outside of marriage, flirts with men or dresses in a provocative manner then she causes shame. Thus female shame could cause male shame since it implies that her male relatives are too weak to control or defend her.[4]

The British Muslim author Mohammad Raza claims that this concept of *izzat* – the male domination and female submission syndrome, the female sexual distrust syndrome, the female as property syndrome – all are deeply rooted in the Muslim's patriarchal culture.[5] He says that there is an inherent basic distrust of womanhood and its sexuality. This emanates from the view that a woman is considered as "property" rather than as a person. Property must be safeguarded for if it is "damaged" through sexual contact it can bring "dishonor" and "shame" on the family. According to this concept, the woman in a family, through proper behaviour brings honor to the men of the family so that their honor and prestige (and secondarily that of the woman) are maintained, if not enhanced.[6]

One family told me that if their daughter was being beaten in a marriage they would do nothing about it, as it could bring shame on the entire family. They would rather keep their honor and let their daughter suffer. As long as it was hidden from the outside world that would satisfy them.

It is quite common for Muslim girls to leave school at sixteen and stay at home to look after the house and family. Many are not permitted to go to university or to have any further education. The parents see this as protection for the girl, ensuring that no harm will come to her and she will be pure and a virgin when she marries. This will also ensure that she will not have a child outside of marriage, which is the ultimate shame. This would not only reflect badly on her but on the people who were supposed to be controlling her. Any action that defied the elder generation's authority to control her sexual rights was deemed to be shameful. A marriage will usually be arranged as soon as possible after leaving school or further education.

The excessive zeal with which women must be guarded and their virginity protected makes them an almost intolerable burden on the family which, naturally, makes it a point to find husbands for them and to hand them over to their in-laws as soon as possible. A daughter is always regarded as a guest in her father's house and her whole training and orientation is only to be a good wife and daughter-in-law and learn to obey.[7]

Curbing Female Sexuality

Curbing active female sexuality is the basis of many of Islam's family institutions. The stability of society is maintained by creating institutions which encourage men to dominate within it, while secluding women from it. Islamic laws are therefore saturated by a notion of the eminence of men over women, and they include numerous rules to regulate women's lives.[8]

Islam perceives women as a disruptive force. There appears to be an assumption that men cannot resist women's lure, which offers a justification for controlling their sexuality. The solution to the problem of what is seen as women's disruptive power is to confine her to the home where she has to look after the children and to enforce the use of the veil.[9] Ghazali, one of Islam's classical scholars on marriage, sees civilisation struggling to contain women's destructive, all absorbing power. He believes women exert a fatal attraction which erodes the male's will to resist her and places him in a passive and pliable role.

This power is seen as the most destructive element in the Muslim social order, because men become distracted from their social and religious duties. Society can only survive by creating institutions that foster male dominance through sexual segregation and polygamy. He casts the woman as the hunter and the man as the passive victim.[10]

It is reported that once when Muhammad saw a woman, he hurried to his house and had intercourse with his wife Zaynab. He then left the house and said, 'The woman advances and returns in the shape of a devil.'[11]

It is because of this view of women that Islam traditionally has separate places for men and women. Women ideally only speak to women apart from male relatives. It is similar with the men, as they only speak to men apart from female members of their own household. With the younger generation these strict codes are breaking down due partly to mixed sex schools and the social codes in places of higher education.

Honor Killings

Honor killing has its roots in the crude Arabic expression "a man's honor lies between the legs of a woman". For Muslim women, virginity before marriage and fidelity afterwards are considered musts and men are expected to control their female relatives. If a woman strays, it is widely thought that the dignity of the man can be restored only by killing her. The slightest sniff of scandal can be a death warrant. Often, honor killings are carried out on the flimsiest of grounds, such as a man claiming he dreamt his wife had betrayed him. Communities are almost always supportive of these murders. Women have endured the custom while legal establishments have tolerated or even condoned it.[12] In Pakistan, convicted perpetrators of murders linked to family honor are generally given lighter sentences than other killers, as the law often makes provision for reduced sentences in cases where honor is involved. In some cases men have been jailed for as little as three months, in others they have never been brought to justice.[13]

There are an increasing number of these honor killings reported every year in western countries. Currently there are about twenty honor killings a year in the United Kingdom, and there are fears that the number will increase. The Metropolitan Police Service has formed a task force to increase its understanding of "honor killings," to help them investigate the murders and better help those who may be at risk.[14]

In countries like Pakistan there are hundreds of honor killings every year. The murders are usually exceptionally brutal with the perpetrators often employing knives, axes and even guns. Honor killings are male gender based violence, which can be perpetrated by cousins, fathers, brothers, uncles, sons or any male relative against a female member of the family. A son can kill his mother if he believes that she is having an affair, though there might be no proof of it. A father can kill his daughter. The reason is simply that they believe the woman has stepped out of line with her behaviour, perhaps by refusing an arranged marriage, or by what she wears or by sexual misconduct. They believe that she must be punished to restore the family honor.

In Britain, while the prevailing culture in the Muslim community favours honor killing, some Muslim leaders have opposed it. They have argued that the practice is un-Islamic. A spokesman for the Muslim Council of Britain has stated, "Islam categorically does not allow anyone to kill their own daughter".[15]

Honor killings are routed in the old patriarchal system and are as old as the history of Islam. They took place long before the modern day clash of cultures. However in the West the trigger can be a clash of cultures between East and West, the old and the young.

Many parents who come from strict religious backgrounds are scandalised by what they see as the uncontrollable behaviour of their children. Threats, beatings and the lurking possibility of the ultimate sanction are used as a means of control.

The Yones Family

The Yones family arrived in Britain in 1993 from northern Iraq. Their daughter Heshu mixed with friends from all cultures. Her father grew increasingly distressed that she was not living according to Muslim values. He tried to beat her into submission but she continued to wear pretty dresses and enjoy a social life. She attempted to placate him by dressing down at home and putting on make-up only when she was away from the family. However she remained terrified that her father would discover that she had a boyfriend. Her letters found later showed that she was planning to run away from home and to start a new life. In one of the letters she told her father that she wanted to be alone and that he should not try to track her down.

When an anonymous letter arrived revealing that his daughter had slept with her boyfriend, his worst fears were confirmed. In a rage he confronted his daughter, slit her throat and continually stabbed her. He was horrified at what he believed was a stain on the family's name and was desperate to restore his honor, which he believed could only be done by killing her. Many such men have no fear of the law and are convinced such killings are an acceptable way to avenge damaged family honor. They may collude with other family members to kill.[16]

These crimes are an ever increasing phenomenon in multicultural Britain and such is the protective nature of the families and communities in which they occur that outsiders rarely become aware of the victim's sufferings. If they do intervene it is invariably too late. Most honor killings are characterised by extreme secrecy.[17]

Rita Rupal, director of the Newham Asian Women's project has found that living in the West actually reinforces traditional values. Communities feel threatened because of factors such as racism and become more tightly knit. Their cultural identity becomes fixed and does not change as it normally would, because they feel threatened by what they see around them.[18] Muslim young women are not usually free to act in any way they please as their culture demands a high degree of conformity; wherever they go they represent families and communities and must guard the reputation of those families and communities.

Honor Suicides

Until recently in Turkey, a man who killed his female kin for reasons of honor or tradition was treated leniently. Often a young brother, who was a minor would own up to a murder and would be let off with little more than a slap on the wrist. The killings and what was effectively legal collusion, figured in the EU reports on the progress of its latest candidate country. In 2005 the Turkish law was changed regarding "honor killings". Turkey now gives life imprisonment to family members and those who take part in "honor killings". By May of 2006, thirty-six women had committed suicide in Turkey which was more than all of last year. The general suicide rate in Turkey is low compared to the rest of the world but the nature of these deaths was very different. Women's groups believe that the errant women are being told "Here's a gun or here is some poison go and kill yourself so I don't have to go to prison for it." If they don't comply they are killed anyway and declared to have committed suicide after a bout of depression.[19]

Islamic Marriage in the West

Arranged marriages are the norm within the Muslim community even in western countries. When a marriage is arranged it is a contract between two families and not two individuals. It is usually arranged between family members who may later use family pressure to ensure its survival. As soon as a daughter has finished school, often at age 16 or after higher education, she will have a marriage arranged for her, usually with a man from the parent's country of origin. The person most likely will be a relative, usually a first cousin or someone more distant within the family. They can be totally uneducated, which can produce enormous tensions within a marriage, as they will be from a different class and culture from the wife.

I came across this in a girl of Indian origin who was born in Britain. She had been trained as a hairdresser and had a marriage arranged with a manual worker from India. She shared with me how unsatisfactory this was because their thoughts, ideals and general lifestyle were completely different. They were two different people from different worlds. What she had wanted was a modern western-style marriage. The question that faces her now is - can the marriage last?

Some of the girls I interviewed would like to choose their own marriage partners, but in the final analysis said that they would leave it to their parents. However one of the girls is determined to marry someone who was born in Britain. They do believe their parents would choose someone that they could love. The question is whether, when the time comes to accept an arranged marriage, they will be willing to do so. However, sometimes girls who have been educated at university and are a little older, do find the courage they didn't realise they had.

The eighteen-year-old girl mentioned in the previous chapter who was betrothed at the age of five would be relieved to marry almost anyone else, as she does not want to marry the man to whom she has been promised. Her refusal to marry him is causing conflict within the home, and what she really wants is to be able to choose her own husband. This issue was raised by both the husband and wife when I spoke to them and had become a burden and a cause of anguish for them. To not honor the commitment was unthinkable. It seems likely from what the parents have said that through subtle pressure the girl will be forced to marry this person. Another family mentioned that they had chosen the husband for their older daughter from Pakistan and would be choosing the husband for their younger daughter.

One girl told me that when she had gone to Bangladesh for her sister's wedding, not realising that she was going to be married at the same time as her sister. She felt she was forced into a marriage that she didn't want, but being in Bangladesh all she could do was to submit, albeit unwillingly. She was extremely upset about it but said that there was nothing she was able to do in the circumstances. She appears now to be under severe stress and tension.

Husbands which are not Acceptable

It can be very difficult for girls to choose their own marriage partner. If the man they wish to marry is not a Muslim, the majority of parents will oppose it absolutely. The young person who does this will have to bear the consequences, which may mean being cut off completely from the family. They will have to leave home and may never see their parents again. For a young man even if he converts to Islam it makes little difference, as this has brought shame on the family.

If the man they want to marry is a fellow Muslim it is still generally unacceptable as the person will not be known to the family. There is nothing worse that the girl could have done, as it has brought shame on the family in the face of the whole community. This was the fear expressed by all of the mothers with teenage children. Half of the mothers said that if this happened to their daughter they would not cut them off from the family. However when it becomes a reality the family often find it difficult to cope and acceptance does not come readily. All the girls I interviewed said they knew girls who had run away and got married, and in each case the family had cut them off. One girl said that she knew seven girls who had done this. I questioned the number and she told me again seven.

The Story of Yasmin and Khalid

In the British Muslim magazine Q News there was a story about a girl called Yasmin who married her cousin Khalid from Pakistan. Yasmin had been earmarked for Khalid on the day she was born and it was always drummed into her that she would be marrying her cousin. Nobody considered an alternative. She said it was though she was already married to him and only the formalities remained. These formalities took place when Yasmin went to Pakistan in 1989. She did not dare to protest as she had no idea that she had a choice in the situation, and was too scared to speak out against her parents.

However for ten years now she has carried on a secret relationship with a non-Muslim called Tony, whom she met at her work. Yasmin always thought that the submission Islam required of her was that of surrendering to the will of her parents. She was always led to believe that being a good Muslim was about pleasing one's parents and she had no idea of her right to object if she didn't consent. If only she had known, she would not have consented to the wedding. She said that the day she got married to Khalid all she could think was of Tony. Yasmin insists she was never told about her right to object if she didn't consent to the marriage, or encouraged to study Islam for herself, but was always expected to take her parents word for it. She believed her parents' held an extreme and unappealing view of Islam. In rejecting her parents' views she has adopted her own interpretation of Islam which no longer stops her from marrying the man she loves. She says that she doesn't feel that Allah will hate her for it, as Islam does not insist on arranged marriages or on marrying someone you do not love.

Yasmin said that when she began to fall in love with Tony she started to become conscious of the fact that their differences would pose a problem. She said that she had tried to concentrate on her marriage and prevent this relationship as much as possible, but it was because of what she suffered with Khalid that things became serious between her and Tony. She said that she had been forced to go back to work because Khalid was too lazy to work himself. The more she found lacking in Khalid the more she turned to Tony.

The financial burden had been left on Yasmin as Khalid could not support her and their child. He had never been to school in Pakistan and so did not know any English, and he thought that when he came to Britain he would not have to work. He considered that it was Yasmin's duty to provide for him. He could not find a well-paid job and would not consider working in a factory or restaurant. He got so used to the idea of her earning and him spending that he never took his jobs seriously. He had no sense of responsibility as a husband or as a father.

So who does she blame for her predicament? She says, "Our parents' traditional attitudes, their cultural values, their family honor, their stubbornness to let go of the traditions that don't do anything for anyone living in Britain. If a girl stands up for her rights she brings shame on the family. These old fashioned ideas are what oppress Muslim girls, not Islam. This is the whole problem. I was brought up as a good obedient Pakistani girl, not as a good Muslim. I know there are restrictions for women in Islam but there are also rights which Muslim culture takes away. Now that Muslim women are going out into the world and meeting men of other cultures they are realising that not all men are the same and that they don't have to live life in the same submissive way that their mothers did".

She said that all that mattered to her parents was that he was family and that meant not having to spend large amounts on the dowry or on all the other expenses of a wedding. It didn't matter to her parents that he was uneducated, did not want to work and was brought up in a village with traditional ideas. Yasmin describes her marriage as one of convenience that was convenient for everyone except the bride.[1]

Forced Marriages

There is an important difference between arranged and forced marriages. Many girls accept an arranged marriage and appear to have no difficulty with it. Many just go along with an arranged marriage and are too fearful to stand against it. In my interviews I came across one forced marriage with the possibility of a second.

Forced marriage is a marriage conducted without the valid consent of both parties, where duress is a factor. It is an abuse of fundamental rights and a form of domestic violence which cannot be justified on religious or cultural grounds. Victims tend to be between the ages of 15 and 30. Many parents use religious rationale to justify their use of force and violence. They can be motivated by a desire to strengthen family links, to protect cultural and religious ideals, to prevent unsuitable relationships and to provide relatives with a passport to life in the West.[2] An estimated 70% of forced marriages end in divorce, according to Ghayasuddin Siddiqui, leader of the Muslim Parliament of Britain.

Every year there are hundreds of Muslim girls in Britain being forced into marriage. Research commissioned by Scotland's Pakistani community found that almost half of marriages involving Scottish Muslims and a partner from abroad involve coercion.[3] In March 2004, social workers in the UK were issued with guidelines to help them tackle cases involving forced marriage.[4] In the same month the Law Society provided guidelines to solicitors to help them deal with the issue "sensitively but robustly".[5]

As second generation British Muslims demand the right to choose a partner, clashes between traditionalist parents and modern children are resulting in more women being forced and threatened into marrying against their will.[6] It is a classic story, according to Muslim women's groups, civil rights campaigners and community workers, who are witnessing a growing number of young Muslims in turmoil. In some cases, pressure is enough to persuade daughters to go through with the marriage; in others, they are "tricked" into it, believing they are simply going to be taking a holiday or visiting a sick relative in Pakistan. In a few cases they are physically "helped" - perhaps drugged - on to aeroplanes.[7]

Judge annuls Forced Marriage

One girl was subjected to moral blackmail by her parents who threatened to kill themselves if she did not marry the cousin that she had never met. She was kept in a remote part of Pakistan for many months and despite begging her parents to be allowed to return to this country, she was subjected to unrelenting pressure initially from her mother and subsequently by her father, as well as from other members of the wider family. Her passport was taken from her and she was told that she could not return to the UK until she went through with the marriage. She finally married her cousin when she was seventeen.

When she applied to have the marriage annulled the judge said "In my judgement she is not bound by the ceremony. She did not validly consent. She is entitled to the *decree nisi* of nullity which she seeks". She had lived with her husband for a short time before returning to the UK with her parents. The marriage was never consummated and he had admitted to her that it was just a "ploy" to allow him to enter the UK.

The judge added that forced marriage is a gross abuse of human rights. It is a form of domestic violence that dehumanises people by denying them their right to choose how to live their lives. It is an appalling practice. He added "No social or cultural imperative can extenuate and no pretended recourse to religious belief can possibly justify forced marriage. Forced marriage is intolerable. It is an abomination".[8]

Many when married are forced to live in remote underdeveloped villages with no access to phones or computers. They are watched day and night and put under psychological and violent pressure from the family. Once married many are raped and beaten.[9]

Men and Forced Marriage

Men are also the hidden victims of forced marriages, and make up about 15% of those rescued from abroad. They are often emotionally blackmailed into giving their consent. If they changed their minds once they got abroad, they found they were trapped as their passports were taken away from them until they consented to marry the woman.[10]

New Domestic Violence Laws

At the beginning of 2008 there was a case in the UK courts where the relatives of a teenage bride, Sabia Rani, turned a blind eye as she was beaten to death by her husband, Shazad Khan. They will now face up to 14 years in jail. Three women, her mother-law and two sisters-in-law, and her sister-in law's husband were convicted under the new domestic violence laws for failing to step in. Her husband had been jailed one year previous to the court case. Sabia was attacked over a three week period, suffering "catastrophic" injuries usually only seen in car crash victims. The young vulnerable 19 year old, who had arrived five months earlier from Pakistan for the arranged marriage, should have been taken to hospital for emergency treatment in an intensive care unit. None of the in-laws she lived with helped her and she was left to die at home. The case was one of the first under the new laws which allow for the prosecution of someone not directly involved with a child or "vulnerable", adults death, but should have intervened to stop it. This law will prove to be a new departure in obtaining justice for honor killings.[11]

Forbidden Love

The BBC broadcast a television programme in 1998 on this subject called "Forbidden Love". It stated that a family would do everything possible to stop a daughter marrying outside the community, as it would bring shame on the family. The subject was never discussed as it was too shameful. The film went on to show that in a situation like this, the parents and family would issue threats. If the young person still wanted to live their own life the family would disown them and that meant complete severance with the family. In some cases they would attempt to send their daughter to their country of origin and have her married off there, on the pretext of sending them for a holiday. There are some cases where the family feels that they are so shamed and embarrassed that it becomes a vendetta, and there are cases where they will go to any lengths even murder.[12]

Amar and Aneeka

An article appeared in The Sunday Times in 1994 about a couple called Amar and Aneeka who met at college and wanted to marry. Her parents, unhappy at her choice, took her to Bangladesh and forced her to marry a man there. She is still there against her will. The article goes on to say that "the objection to their friendship is cultural. Although both are from Yorkshire and Muslim, her family is from Bangladesh, his from Pakistan. It's fear of what other people think. Amar explains the culture without resentment. Aneeka is the oldest girl in her family and it is important she marries well. When she announced that she wanted to marry Amar, their beating put her in hospital. The traditional answer is to run away, as hundreds of Britain's Asian teenagers do every year".

In a letter Aneeka managed to get to Amar through a sympathetic uncle, she wrote, "At this moment what hurts me is that I am another victim. You know, I know, it has happened to so many girls. I'm now one of them. I'm ashamed".[13]

The Reasons for Forced Marriage

The reasons for forced marriages are complex but the analysis does show that sexuality and independence amongst young women can trigger off a forced marriage. Parents interpret their daughter's desire to go to university as a sign that they would end in an unacceptable relationship with someone from outside their own community. Forcing them into a marriage of their parents' choice is sometimes seen as a way of pre-empting such an eventuality.[14]

All the older women that I interviewed said they would bring a husband for their daughter from their country of origin. Why do so many Muslim parents go back home to look for a match when there are so many young people from their race and religion here in Britain? A social historian specialising in Asian families has said that many families, especially lower middle and working classes, are "both backward and insular". For some it is as though they never left India or Pakistan or wherever they came from. Streets in Birmingham, Bradford or East London may look the same as back home and the life inside the same as well. Old customs are preserved as if their lives depended on it, and these include sexual taboos and marriage traditions.

Girls running away from Muslim homes are an increasing problem. It is very common for girls to leave home to escape an arranged marriage or because they have boyfriends their families may not approve of.

Jack and Zena

Jack and Zena are a couple who have been in hiding for over five years. During these years they have moved nineteen times. Every time they go inside their home they place heavy furniture against the front door and put a knife within quick reach. Zena (not her real name) is now 25, and the Englishman she married is 35 and goes by the name of Jack. Zena is the British born daughter of Pakistani immigrants and is under a death threat from her own father and brother. They have vowed to find her and murder her because she left home refusing to give up her studies and accept an arranged marriage with a man they chose from a Pakistani village.[15]

In 2006 eight years after the above paragraph was written, an article appeared in the Sunday Times in the UK. It stated that Jack and Zena had been given the all-clear by Special Branch. The police had decided that there was no longer "any credible threat to their lives". However that didn't mean that they were going back to their home town of Leeds or revealing where they were going to live. This has been after three sets of name changes and one complete identity change. They are aware that the threat is still there to some degree, and the dream of a simple normal life is still some way off.[16]

Bounty Hunters

Police forces, community workers, and women's groups report an increase in young women running away to avoid arranged marriages. Some are found by family and friends, others are ruthlessly tracked down by bounty hunters hired by families who pay as much as three thousand pounds plus expenses for the return of their daughter. The bounty hunters show no remorse as they only want the money. Muslim women's groups are setting up increasing numbers of refuges throughout the country to help such runaways.[17]

The women who are being pursued cannot identify who is coming after them until it is too late. Families will never admit hiring bounty hunters and the women who are forcibly taken to Pakistan, even if they are British born, fall out of British jurisdiction once they are back in their parent's native land.[18]

Proof of Virginity

The Arabic word for virgin is a feminine noun which always refers to women. There is no masculine equivalent. Great lengths are taken by parents to protect their daughter's virginity. Every Muslim girl is expected to be a virgin on her wedding night, and later is expected never to be involved in extra-marital relationships. The same restrictions do not apply to men, considerable numbers at some stage in their life visit prostitutes with comparative freedom. It is no loss to a man's honor to sleep with a prostitute for she is considered to be nothing. This makes a considerable double standard with regard to the sexual behaviour between men and women.[19]

In traditional Muslim societies virginity is flouted after the marriage. Blood alone is the mark of the intact honor (hymen) on the wedding night. In a traditional setting, the midwife would be there with the sharp instrument to plunge into the membrane, blood would pour out. The showing in public of a blood spotted cloth brings honor to the family, and a celebration follows.

But if a girl is not a virgin there are alternative ways to produce the evidence that would make the difference between honor and dishonor, between living and dying. Women resort to filling their vaginas with blood soaked sponges or splinters of glass to compensate for lost hymens. If a couple had pre-marital sex, the husband might cut himself on the wedding night to produce blood to conceal the failure of the virginity test. In some cases a medical doctor will provide proof of virginity for a fee,[20] or perform an operation to repair a torn hymen. If a bride is found not to be a virgin she can be returned to her family, who, in traditional communities, can kill her to restore their honor. This is seen as justified.

In the UK women are being given "virginity repair" operations on the National Health System. Official figures reveal that there were 24 hymen replacement operations between 2005 and 2006. Also an increasing number of women are paying up to £4,000 in private clinics for the procedure, apparently under pressure from future spouses or in-laws who believe they should be virgins on their wedding night. The demand for this operation is increasing, particularly from UK residents. The trend has been condemned by critics as a sign of social regression driven by Islamic fundamentalists. Some countries have made hymen reconstruction illegal.[21]

Polygamy

The marriage and divorce laws in Islam have a profound effect on the family unit, which impact on the society. In Islam a man is permitted to have up to four wives at one time, a woman only one husband. The fear of a husband taking another wife causes the Muslim woman to have insecurity in the marriage. This creates a setting for women to always distrust their husbands. A Muslim woman cannot rely on her husband's loyalty to her in a marriage and will be threatened by any woman be it single or otherwise who comes near her husband. Because the loyalty to the husband is undermined, a Muslim woman may change her loyalty to her family and her first born son. The son then becomes her defender even against his own father. If a problem arises in the marriage the wife goes to her father or brother to settle the dispute with the husband. A Muslim man is loyal to his other wives and to his own family who cover up for him. Therefore the whole social structure becomes distorted.

Polygamy in the UK

Polygamy is allowed in many Muslim countries but is prohibited in the UK. However behind the scenes polygamy is occurring. The second marriage takes place with only a religious ceremony at a mosque that is not registered for civil marriage (in the UK only 160 mosques out of 1500 are registered for civil marriage). This marriage is conducted under Shari'a Law, with no accompanying civil law ceremony which has enormous implications if the marriage fails. The husband can then divorce her under Shari'a Law by simply saying "I divorce you," three times. The woman has very little rights if she is a second wife and living in the UK, and many such women have left the marriage with absolutely nothing. They would only have the status of a mistress. Women have no equivalent right of divorce under Shari'a Law. Or the husband might get a second wife by making a visit to his country of origin where he would marry. He would not bring this wife to the UK but just visit her from time to time.

Because Britain does not allow polygamy this raises problems for Muslim residents of the UK who contracted polygamous marriages either before their emigration or while on a visit to their home country. The Muslim Parliament of Britain has complained that many families are being forced to live outside of the law because their polygamous marriages are not being recognised in the United Kingdom. One estimate gives the number of polygamous families in Britain at several hundreds.[22]

Polygamy is only supposed to occur with the consent of the other wife or wives. However in reality this rarely happens. A British Muslim woman who had been married for thirty years discovered that her husband, on a visit to Pakistan, had married a twenty-six-year-old cousin without her knowledge or consent. She was devastated, but felt that she had no choice but to accept the situation.[23]

In another case, a Muslim woman from a poor background in Pakistan accepted the offer of an arranged marriage to an older man in the United Kingdom. Shortly after her arrival her husband died leaving her in poverty. A rich businessman whose wife was ill and infertile offered to make her his second wife, and married her in a Muslim ceremony.

She moved in with him and had two children. The first wife, in a fit of jealousy, threw her out with her two children. The Muslim community treated her as a shameful loose woman with illegitimate children, and the man stopped paying her maintenance. The poor woman however had no access to the courts to demand maintenance as a legal wife.[24]

Polygamy causes great pain and suffering and dissension within a family and leaves women in a very weak position. It also has damaging consequences in the bringing up of the children. Out of all the girls I interviewed none of them wanted to be in a polygamous situation.

Muslim Women in the West

Divorce and Muslim Women

All the women I interviewed knew of fellow Muslims who had been through divorce. Girls who are educated in Britain are aware of their rights regarding divorce. There is now a high divorce rate amongst Muslim young people, and in 75% of all Muslim divorces it is the women, both young and old, who are divorcing the men. If the woman initiates the divorce there is one in ten chance that they will reconcile, whereas if it is the man who initiates the divorce, nine out of ten women reconcile.[1]

The high proportion of divorces initiated by Muslim women in the UK is notable, as in traditional Muslim societies it is difficult for women to obtain a divorce. In Muslim countries that have Islamic law a woman who divorces her husband must give up her children, who will live with their father or his family. In the countries where this is applied, concern for her children causes women to stay with their husbands, however violent, unfaithful or unreasonable they may be.

It is considered to be a very shameful action when a woman initiates a divorce, and it will affect the whole extended family. The wife will normally have to go back to her own family and is then an outcast in society. If she has no extended family she is very isolated and lost. The older woman may have poor English and be uneducated, and it can be very traumatic.

Reasons for Divorce

It is not considered shameful for a man to divorce, whatever the reason he gives. One legitimate reason considered for divorce is because the wife cannot produce boys. It is a common custom in Muslim societies for the husband to threaten divorce without really intending to go through with it. This is a means whereby the wife is kept under control.

The high divorce rate among Muslims in the UK is often as a result of an arranged or forced marriage and is most prevalent in the 20 to 30 age groups. The major reason that was put forward was that women wanted to choose their own marriage partners. In my interviews, one couple was on the verge of divorce. The girl born in the UK who had married a man from India discussed this with me in detail. She said that the cultural differences between them were too great and they had nothing in common. The marriage was just not working.

One of my interviews was with a 35 year-old Pakistani Muslim woman. Her husband came to Britain when he was seven years old and was 22 when they got married. She came from Lahore to marry him in an arranged marriage. He ran a shop with his brother one hundred miles from London, and returned home only at weekends. In 1991 her husband took her and their three children then aged eight, ten and twelve, two boys and a girl, back to Pakistan where they lived with his family. He returned to Britain. In 1996 he threw her out of the family home in Pakistan with absolutely nothing, not even a passport or any means of identification. Since that day she has not been able to see her children. Her husband has divorced her through the Pakistani Shari'a Law Courts and is now divorcing her through the British courts for desertion of the family. However through her family she has been able to return to Britain. She believes that her husband is planning to take another wife.

For a divorce to be legal in British Law a "decree absolute" must be obtained from a civil court; an Islamic divorce procedure is not enough. Some Muslim women remarry thinking a Muslim divorce is recognised by British law, perhaps as a result of bad advice given by lawyers unaware of key differences between Islamic and British law. When they remarry they are actually committing bigamy, an offence punishable by seven years in prison.[2]

Divorce amongst the Older Generation

Their children have grown up and they have been married for decades. There are an increasing number of Muslim couples who have been married for 25 years or more splitting up. Many of these women are citing infidelity. Lawyers are saying that older men are straying because they have more money.

For the older woman divorce can be a bitter pill to swallow, and many feel very depressed after it comes through, with some suicidal. One woman of 56 said that she felt happy after her divorce. She found that her husband had been visiting nightclubs after calling a strange number she found in his bag. She said that being his wife was a waste of her life, and she now lives for her children and herself. Another woman of 46 had a woman in her late 20's turn up at her home and confront her husband. The young woman asked the husband point-blank if he loved her, and he nodded that he did. The wife's world went tumbling down. She started divorce proceedings because, she said, it is better to be alone than to cry all day.[3]

The Complexities of Muslim Divorce

A recent case shows the complexities of women wanting a divorce that is legal in both civil law and in the eyes of the Muslim community. A Muslim woman was married both in a Muslim and a civil ceremony. She then sought a divorce in both civil and Muslim courts and pursued a civil claim for the return of her dowry in a civil court. This case took years and the woman had to do much of the legal research herself. The civil judge did not recognise her right as a British citizen to have her religious claim heard. Both sides had to employ a single joint expert in Islamic law in the civil case which dragged on for six years until she finally received a "decree absolute" and won costs against her former husband. Following the civil case she petitioned for a Muslim divorce at the Muslim Law (Shari'a) Council (MLSC) in London. This was finally granted in spite of her husband's refusal. Dr Zaki Badawi in his report on the case stated that the husband's stance was "an unacceptable form of blackmail and proof of the intention to harm the interests of the wife". The woman had to endure very lengthy judicial wrangling both in the civil and Islamic court. Her aim was to make her divorce and the payment she received valid in the eyes of the Muslim community as well as the civil legal system. This case exemplifies the many hurdles Muslim women face in claiming their rights.[4]

British law recognises Muslim marriages that were performed abroad before the partners entered the UK. In the UK many Muslims are getting married in a mosque with a Shari'a or Islamic marriage and no accompanying British civil law ceremony. There has been an increase in this practice when it was thought that it would be decreasing with women becoming more educated and aware of their rights. Those affected are often the professionals such as solicitors and accountants. Islamic or Shari'a weddings leave women unprotected, as an Islamic wedding certificate often records a token settlement such as £50 in the event of marriage breakdown. The leader of the self-styled Muslim Parliament of Britain has warned that many women are legally unprotected when their marriages end because they wrongly believe that Islamic wedding ceremonies are recognised by British Law. This is not the case as a Shari'a marriage has to be accompanied by a British Civil Law ceremony to make it a legal marriage in the UK. This means that women only married under Shari'a in the UK can be left with minimal rights on divorce or the death of their partner. Legal experts compared the situation to the widespread but unfounded belief in "common law marriage" when in fact cohabitees have far less rights than spouses. Women are often promised civil ceremonies which never happen. Widows can find that they lack pension rights or any rights to their partner's property if he has not left a will. If the marriage is polygamous only one wife is recognised in the UK. However, British residents in the UK must contract marriage according to civil law in order for the marriage to be legally recognised. Mosques and Islamic centres can be registered with the civil authorities for the solemnisation of marriages, but so far only 160 have done so.[5]

A Muslim solicitor who handles many such cases pleads with Muslim women to ensure a civil registration of their marriage otherwise they will be left with the much lesser rights of a "cohabitee". This solicitor claims that it is very common, even for well-educated Muslim women, to think it unnecessary to register their marriages in the civil system. They then face enormous problems in cases of divorce or death. Many Muslim women in the UK are marrying under Shari'a Law.[6]

Domestic Violence

Some Muslim men accept the idea that it is normal for a man to hit his wife and that she is no more than a piece of his property. Wife abuse has hurt many Muslim women, destroyed many Muslim families and weakened the entire Muslim community. Based on information from grassroot leaders, social workers and activists, at least 10% of British Muslim women are abused emotionally, physically and sexually by their Muslim husbands. Despite the severity of the problem, the Muslim community has largely closed its eyes and devoted very few resources to helping the victims and stopping the abusers. Domestic violence is an ongoing, debilitating experience of physical, psychological, and/or sexual abuse in the home, according to a Muslim social worker.[7]

The most common form of abuse is emotional and mental abuse. The Muslim community tends to dismiss the seriousness of mental abuse, rationalising it as a petty argument between husband and wife, and saying it is not serious until he hits her. In Muslim homes it includes verbal threats to divorce the wife, to remarry, or to take the children away if she does not do exactly as she is told. In reality mental abuse does serious psychological harm to many Muslim women. It destroys their self-esteem and makes them question their self-worth; some have breakdowns and go insane.[8]

Many Muslim women – like many victims of domestic violence of any faith – do not seek out help. They are afraid that if their situation becomes public they will lose their honor because of gossip, and fear that the abusers will get more hostile when the negative publicity gets back to them. Many abused women remain silent because they lack confidence in themselves and believe that they somehow deserve the abuse. They also keep quiet out of a feeling of hopelessness and a belief that no-one will help them, and because of the financial dependence on their husbands or desire to keep the homes together for the children's sake. Other Muslim women accept the abuse as a fact of life and learn to live with it. Of those who reach breaking point and seek help, many Muslim women turn to Imams but often find them unhelpful. Looking for other sources of help many Muslim women turn to relatives only to be told to accept the abuse because making a big deal out of it could hurt the family's honor and reputation.[9]

In desperation many abused Muslim women turn to shelters run by non-Muslims. They are usually taken to one outside their area so they are unable to be found by other family members. Many of these women visit the mosque and are then found by the family members, as it is reported back. Our daughter Ruth ran such a refuge in the centre of London for many years. She was constantly in touch with the police and social workers having to deal with many abusive situations.

The issue still remains a taboo subject among all major Muslim organisations.

Honor-Related Violence

Up to 17,000 women in the UK are being subjected to "honor" related violence every year, according to the Police Chiefs. They warn that the number of girls falling victim to forced marriages, kidnappings, sexual assaults, beatings and even murder by relatives intent on upholding the "honor" of their family is up to 35 times higher than official figures suggest. The crisis with children as young as eleven being sent abroad to be married has prompted the authorities to take more action.[10]

The Domestic Violence Working Group warned that fears of retribution and the failure of the authorities to understand the problem completely meant that the vast majority of victims were too scared to come forward for help. The British authorities are bringing three girls home a week from Pakistan as victims of forced marriage, but recognise that it is the tip of the iceberg. The Governments Forced Marriage Unit (FMU) handled approx. 400 cases in 2007. And it is not only women that are affected, 15% of the cases involve men and boys.[11]

Education

Many young Muslim girls want to go on to further education or take some form of training, but some are forced to leave school at sixteen. Some do go on to take training courses. One girl I met trained as a hairdresser, one had done a year's business course, and another a two-year community course. These three girls had all worked up to the time of marriage and beyond. They had continued working after the marriage until their husbands arrived in the UK, which usually took about 18 months to two years. They were required to work for this period by the immigration authorities, to show that there was an income coming in. These and other girls fitted into the pattern of the parents from a rural background taking their girls out of school at 16, where they would either stay at home or go out to work until they were married. Husbands would be found from the country of origin. After they are married or when their husbands arrived in the country they then had to stay at home. When I met these three girls they were not working but desperately wanted to.

However, one girl I met from this socio-economic group had managed to go to university. Others were very keen to do so. Girls from middle-class backgrounds usually do go on to some form of training or further education. However it is not usual for a girl to go away to university, but will find a course where she can live at home. If she has to go away she will in most cases stay with relatives.

Leading a Double Life

The young people I spoke to said that many Muslim girls go into further education for the specific reason of having more freedom. They see it as the only time in their life when they can choose to do as they please. They may travel to university in *hijab* or conservative

Muslim dress and remove it as soon as they get there. They usually adopt some form of western dress rather than traditional clothing.

Many are leading a double life. The university by day, then one of the student bars at night wearing a sexy dress. And there they party until the early hours, drinking, smoking and experimenting with the typical lifestyle of a British undergraduate. When they go home they revert back to the dutiful daughter. The taste is bittersweet. When they graduate they return to their parent's home where she will resume the life of a "good girl", cocooned in a community where drinking, smoking and having boyfriends is considered sinful. One girl says "During her time at university she has done everything that is forbidden by her religion".[12]

And as more Muslim women go into higher education this double life is becoming something of a hidden social phenomenon. Many of these women believe that they are part of a "limbo", generation. Not content to play out the uneducated, subservient roles that many of their mothers did, they are searching for a way to balance their inherited religious and cultural beliefs with those of western society. Some look back and see it as fun, and see no contradiction in taking a couple of years off from tradition to do what their friends are doing, whilst others struggle with the double life. Some young women after university manage to get this "thirst for freedom", out of their system and settle down to married life. Some can never forgo their new life. And ironically these women are only experiencing what their brothers have been doing for years. It's almost an accepted rite of passage that men go to university and live it up before returning home to settle down with a nice Muslim girl. One woman said that she cried for a month when her university course ended and was convinced that she would be married off within a year. Three years after leaving university she is still living with her parents and working.[13]

The double life takes its toll on some Muslim girls, and they are almost overcome with feelings of guilt and paranoia. Some have nervous breakdowns. It is a sense of restlessness from being shielded and over-protected that encourages these girls to try this side of life. But one thing these women are insistent on is that they will keep their wild university days to their husband a secret.[14]

The Tensions caused by Wearing Western Dress

All the girls I interviewed were wearing western dress, and said that they wore western clothes for school and when they go out with their friends. Half of the older women were also wearing western dress. In fact Muslim girls are dressing in ways very similar to their western counterparts, except that their clothes are in many cases being bought through the Asian shops which show some contextualisation to an Asian Muslim youth culture, for example with denim skirts being ankle-length and T-shirts having long sleeves. They would only wear their traditional dress when they visit with their family or on a special occasion.

In a survey carried out of young Muslims in Britain, attitudes to the question, "Do you see anything wrong with Muslim girls wearing western clothes?" were extremely varied. Young people were less likely to see anything wrong than the parents.[15] The question of dress is considered to be relevant to religion. The thinking is that western clothes are not considered to be acceptable by the older generations and that Muslim cultural conditions do not permit them to be worn.

Careers and Muslim Women

Research into the career destinations of Muslim women from 1995-1998, by Professor Marie Parker Jenkins of the University of Derby, examined their school and post-school experiences, family backgrounds, personal attitudes to work and self-motivation and their role in affecting career opportunities. The report claimed that it is twice as hard for Muslim women to succeed in achieving their career goals because of "hostility" from college, discrimination at work and struggles within their communities.[16]

All the girls and young women I interviewed who were under 30 wanted to work, and some wanted to have serious careers. However they said that there are many obstacles in the way. One of the major obstacles is the husband who has come from overseas, who espouses traditional conservative cultural values. There are also other obstacles. One girl had worked as a doctor's receptionist and is now looking for similar work, but she can only get it at a very low salary. She will have to look for other work. She has the added difficulty in finding childcare for her two year old daughter. She does not want her mother to look after the child as she is fearful that the child will be closer to her mother than herself.

Muslim girls face a disproportionate amount of pressure from their immediate family, which is often unwilling to support girl's career aspirations out of fear how it will be perceived in the wider community. This causes great frustration with young Muslim girls who have career aspirations, but whose parents say that is not acceptable in their community. Reluctantly they come to the conclusion that there is no point in arguing, because if you rebel you will be disowned.[17]

The report went on to say that a change in parental attitudes could be detected towards girls who work. Possible reasons for this shift are identified as the realisation by Muslim parents that education is necessary for survival, and that Muslim men are increasingly looking for more educated partners.[18]

Religion

Apart from two girls from Saudi Arabia, Islam was very far from the thoughts and minds of all the women and girls I interviewed. It is not compulsory for women to attend the mosque, and in fact the majority of mosques have little provision for them. Women are encouraged instead to pray at home. But none of the Muslim girls and women I interviewed prayed at home. One girl told me that her two-year-old daughter would not know anything about Islam because she knew nothing about it herself. She said that she had never attended a Qur'anic school because there was none in her area.

This situation is something that is changing for many women and girls, which will be discussed in chapter seven.

The Extended Family

Many Muslim young people want to live in a nuclear family when they marry and not an extended family. They want to be independent, but would not mind having their parents living nearby, where they could help look after the children.

There is some evidence that the extended family system may weaken in the future. In the survey referred to above, 58% of young Muslims agreed with the statement "When I have a home of my own, I would prefer to have only my husband/wife and children living with me". The main reasons for preferring to live in a nuclear family were privacy, independence and having their own home.[19]

The Older Generation of Muslim Women

The consensus of the women I interviewed was that in the UK they had much more freedom to move about than in their countries of origin, where they would need a male escort to go outside the home. Here they can go outside the home and do as they please during the day, while their husbands are at work. Two of the older Muslim women mentioned that some Muslim women are even having men friends and visiting them.

Out of all the older women I visited none had worked outside the home after marriage. But they did tell me that more women of a slightly older age group are beginning to go out to work and wear western dress. They said that the husband feels under pressure when he thinks his wife is becoming westernised, and this can lead to arguments in the home.

I was very surprised to find that about half of the older women I visited were wearing western dress – trousers and a top - during the interview, rather than their traditional dress. This would be unusual in their countries of origin.

None of the older women would be drawn to comment on violence in the home. The younger women who were not married said that they were very concerned about it. The Christian woman in charge of a refuge in East London told me that based on her experience violence was common within Muslim homes.

Female Genital Mutilation

The practice of female genital mutilation is very common in the Muslim community in many parts of the world. Some Muslim leaders have spoken out to condemn the practice as un-Islamic and culturally bound, but many communities see it as sanctioned by Islam as well as being essential for preserving the woman's chastity and family honor. An estimated 7,000 girls in Britain are at risk from this procedure at any given time. The law is being evaded by families taking the girls abroad for a holiday and having the procedure carried out there. In the UK the Home Office recently introduced new legislation under which parents who take their daughters abroad to undergo FGM will face 14 years in jail.[20]

The Veil

In Turkey (1926) and in Iran (1936) the ruling elites introduced compulsory unveiling to herald the dawning of an era of progress. The veil became the symbol of retardation, backwardness and subjugation. This caused offence to the populations who considered the veil as proper attire. The idea of westerners – or westernised elites – telling Muslim women they should remove the veil, that it was a symbol of oppression, was considered to be a continuation of the colonial attitude that promoted western culture as superior to Muslim culture. The ban of the *hijab* on Turkish campuses brought about student demonstrations and hunger strikes. To understand the obsession with the *hijab* it must be viewed as a coded message that reflects political and ideological choices.[1]

The word *hijab* comes from the Arabic *hijaba* which means to debar, to conceal or hide, as it prevents seeing or beholding.[2] It is considered to be a barrier or curtain to render the woman invisible. There are various schools of thought on how this should be implemented. One school of thought says the *hijab* refers to the covering of the hair and neck only, with what is usually called the (Islamic) headscarf. In some Muslim countries this is the minimum requirement. Of course there are women who don't wear the *hijab*.

Another school of thought says that the woman should be

completely covered including her head, face, hands and feet and other parts of the body. This is called by different names depending on the country, for example *hijab, burqa, chador* or, *niqab*. There are many different kinds of dress worn by Muslim women that may come somewhere between these in terms of concealment.

The Purpose of the Veil

The purpose of the complete covering is to conceal the details of the woman's body and her finery which she uses to enhance her appearance. It must conceal the clothes which are underneath. If it is colourful and decorative, it becomes an ornament in itself and defeats its own purpose. In addition, there are many traditions that forbid women from wearing perfume outside their homes. A woman whose perfume excites a man is herself guilty of adultery.[3]

A Symbol of Radical Islam

The *burqa* has been a symbol that is imposed in situations where Islam has become more "fundamentalist", in fact a symbol of radical Islam. We are familiar with pictures of women under the Taliban in Afghanistan, when all women had to be covered in a thick cloth with a small grille for the eyes. If she accidentally showed her face or ankles she could be arrested.[4]

The Ayatollah Khomeini in Iran imposed the *burqa* after the 1979 revolution and there was a never-ending string of *fatwas* which bit by bit took away the fundamental liberties of women. Soldiers monitored women's clothes, watching out for any touch of make-up or a flash of ankle. Hundreds of women were imprisoned and beaten on the soles of their feet rendering them unable to walk for months. Some were even hanged for transgressions of dress codes.

One woman, the child psychiatrist Homa Darabi, set her veil alight and burnt herself to death in a square in Tehran in 1994.

She was protesting against the imposition of the *burqa* and against other injunctions that had incarcerated Iranian women in the home. At this time Algerian women, especially university students, were being assassinated for not covering themselves properly. In Saudi Arabia today, women who are publicly beaten or beheaded are completely covered. They don't even have the right to show their tears, or look at the sky before their heads roll.[5] In these and other Muslim countries women do not have a choice whether to wear the *burqa* or not, it is compulsory. It is hard to see this as anything other than a symbol of women's inferior status, used to divide men from women and render women literally invisible to all but the family.

It is interesting to observe a woman in complete *burqa* eating a meal in a restaurant. I have seen many such women in various parts of the world including Britain. The woman has to lift the flap with one hand whilst remaining veiled and put the food in with the other hand. It appears very demeaning and to my eyes it seems to highlight the inferior status of the woman.

Many Muslim men believe that by not veiling, especially in countries where Muslims are in a minority, women are harming Muslim society. The reasons they cite are that it is a violation of the Qur'an and Hadith and shows women's weakness in belief, it is a cause of temptation for men and women, it subjects the woman to sexual harassment, hurts her dignity and stains her chastity[6]. Muhammad apparently believed it would be a protection against the sexual temptations that would occur when men and women met, as any contact between men and women would inevitably lead to illicit sexual relations and impure thoughts. He believed that if a man and woman were alone in one place the third person present was the devil.[7]

An Oman-based talk show host, Zawan Al-Said, has said that the female Muslim practice of covering the hair with a *hijab* is enjoying its fifteen minutes of western fame and not merely because the French Parliament has just voted overwhelmingly to pass a Bill prohibiting Muslim headdresses in state schools, but for many other reasons. It boils down to one issue: to cover up or not to cover up.

She goes on to say that she wrote to her father asking whether she had to wear the *hijab* or not. He replied that she could carry on wearing her dungarees. In fact her dungarees were yellow corduroys. She said, "I am the only Omani TV broadcaster to appear on screen if not in bright yellow dungarees then, perhaps equally shockingly, bare-headed. It helps to accept local dress codes. Is it surprising that I have never been offered a position of authority in the media, despite the fact that I am more professional than those who have? Though there has been a sharp increase in favour of the *hijab* over the past ten years, I have neither relented nor repented, despite the *hijab* becoming, in some ways, a fashion accessory. For women who have *"hijabbed"* themselves in recent years, there is no turning back: I know of none who have reverted to exposing their hair in public."[8]

The Reasons Why Muslim Women Veil in Britain

In Britain more and more Muslim women are putting on the *hijab*. What has caused this phenomenon? It started after the Muslim protests at the publication of Salman Rushdie's Satanic Verses, when many Muslim women donned the veil as a statement of solidarity with the Muslim community. It was a source of pride to state they were Muslim at a time of great controversy, and it became a political statement. It was the powerful symbol of the Islamic awakening that was to follow.[9]

The wearing of *hijab* is a symbol of the rejection of western values and of allegiance with the Muslim world. Since more and more Muslims are allying themselves with this position as a result of issues such as the war in Iraq, it is perhaps not so surprising that more and more British Muslim women are deciding to wear some form of veiling.

Many Muslim women claim that the *burqa* is a means by which they can be free of sexual harassment from men. They say that underneath the long flowing robes they have freedom, as they can go unnoticed. They consider themselves invisible.

For some Muslim women, wearing some form of *hijab* makes them feel free to mingle with men in mixed social spaces such as universities or workplaces, while at the same time signalling that they are not sexually available. Many girls will be the first generation of women in their family to be part of mixed, western society in this way, and wearing some form of *hijab* can give them the confidence to do so without feeling they are losing their religious and cultural identity.

Body Image and the *Burqa*

Muslim women often claim that by wearing the veil they are free from the tyranny of the beauty industry and its exploitation of the female body. They do not have to bother if their hair is out of place, or if they have put on weight. On the other hand, many Muslim women are very beauty conscious taking great care with their hair and make-up, and wearing the latest fashions under their *burqa*. In fact Muslim women tend to have their faces much more made-up than their western counterparts. In 2002 researchers in Iran found that women in *hijabs* and *burqas* were as anxious as everyone else about their body image. They found that Iranian women living in Iran had a more pathological relationship with their bodies than Iranian women living in the United States. Muslim women's beauty products are catered for even in places like the Regents Park Mosque in central London, where amongst all the religious books you can find anti-cellulite cream and lines of perfume that are considered to be 'Islamic' simply because they contain no alcohol.[10]

In some parts of the UK the choice to wear the *hijab* has now turned to a directive, whilst simultaneously fashionable alternatives are emerging with some women and girls wearing brightly coloured turbans or designer scarves, logo and all. This in Britain is against the backdrop of young women in Iran, desperate to escape imposed modesty, wear chic scarves in silk and chiffon in many colours, tied so that slips of wayward curls escape. For them, the wearing of these scarves is a form of covert resistance and a means of asserting their autonomy[11]. Their cloaks are tighter and a little shorter and the dress police are out once more venting their force against such innocent pleasures. In Iran younger women are rejecting the idea that they must live and die in shrouds and veils.[12]

Imposition of the Hijab

Journalist Yasmin Alibhai-Brown writes that she feels uneasy when she sees young women and girls wearing the *hijab,* usually in grey, white or black. She is not convinced that these are always free choices made after thought and study.[13] All over Britain there are girls, some as young as three, wearing the *hijab*. This is certainly not a result of free choice but of their parents' decision. The parents' decision then becomes the norm.

Many women in the West find the headscarf deeply problematic and identify very strongly with the women who resist the imposition of the veil in Muslim countries. Women who have fled brutal patriarchal regimes and come to the West have become the most vociferous supporters of the French law to ban headscarves in schools and public service.

Defiance and the Hijab

However, the French restriction on the wearing of *hijab* is likely to result in women putting on the headscarf out of defiance, as it has strong echoes of French colonial policy in Algeria, where the veil became a symbol of resistance against the French occupation. It is also likely to increase Muslim separatism. The first private Muslim school in France was set up in Lille in 2003 as a response to girls being sent home for wearing scarves. Now, young, educated Muslim women in France have decided to start wearing the *hijab*, even though there is no tradition of wearing it within their families, because they have began to identify more strongly with Islam.[14]

Symbol of Oppression

None of the young girls I interviewed was wearing *hijab* though a number of the older women were. Yasmin Alibhai-Brown believes that Muslim women need to stop fooling themselves: this *hijab* and *burqa* is not for religion, only for men to have power over them'.[15]

In some places it is taught that if a Muslim woman fails to wear the *hijab*, she is considered a sinner and disobedient to the divine command. Punishment in the after-life will be inflicted on her.[16]

In parts of Britain the veil is becoming obligatory. Many are embracing it willingly and are wearing it with pride. These women are often the ones who fight secularism so bitterly who would have it that no British Muslim schoolgirl strode to school bare-headed or even bare-faced. Even though they do and say these things, they are privileged as they reap all the benefits of western society, education and equality, which are denied to so many Muslim women worldwide.[17]

It is through subtle pressure that others are adopting it. Young girls are wearing it because it is given to them by their parents, with no free will in the matter. Other girls as young as twelve are deciding that they want to be shrouded from head to foot in black with a tiny slit for the eyes. If worn at school, this puts pressure on other young girls to conform to the same dress code. Teachers at these schools say that without being able to see the face there is no individuality, they couldn't call them by name or see their emotions. They were strangers to them and to their classmates and they were forgotten. They sat in the classroom with us but were not part of us. They were effectively invisible.[18]

What really happens behind the *Burqa*

There has been a marked increase in the wearing of the *burqa* in the UK and they are now a common sight on London streets. Some women are saying that they have been forced to wear the *burqa* to hide the violence that fathers and brothers have done to them. Women and girls are beaten because they will not agree to marriages, and just want a little more independence to go to college, amongst other issues. Not all women in *burqa's* are the walking wounded, but some are, and the tragedy is that it is impossible to pick up the signs. The *burqa* is the next frontier for puritanical Muslims who believe females are dangerous seductresses who must be hidden from sight.[19]

Ali-Brown writes "The *burqa* dehumanises. Why do women defend this retreat into shrouds? When I try to speak to these shrouded women on the street they stare back silently. In a Kebab shop in Southall last week, a woman in a *burqa* sat there passively while her family ate-she couldn't put food into her own mouth"[20].

The *burqa* goes against the principles of individual autonomy and equality between the sexes. In Afghanistan and Iran women fight against wearing it as it is recognised as a symbol of oppression. This symbol of oppression in Islamic countries has become a symbol of oppression in the UK.

Contextualisation and Islam

Freedom

What is meant by freedom? Mohammed Raza, Muslim author of Islam in Britain, claims that "young Muslim women simply have no freedom whatsoever, they have less freedom than male Muslims half their age ... freedom to be a human not an excuse for one, living under restrictions as if her entire teenage life were a forbidden age which she needs help to overcome".[1]

Lack of Freedom for Muslim Girls

Many Muslim girls say that they would always obey their parents and try hard not to upset them. However home life is often very strict for them in comparison with their western counterparts. Even after the age of 18, if they want to go to the cinema or go out shopping they would have to seek the permission of their parents. The answer can be no and they would be expected to obey their parents absolutely. After puberty Muslim girls are closely guarded. According to Mohammed Raza, this guarding of women in a culture which grants its women freedom reflects a distrust originating from their countries of origin. He describes it as almost similar to the phobia of Medieval England when crusaders used 'chastity belts' on their women to preserve their virtue.[2]

A Muslim girl is expected to be obedient and subservient to the wishes of the family. Any expression of self-opinion is considered to threaten the power of the patriarchal household. This again conflicts with the norms of British society where individualism is considered a prime quality to be found in a person.[3]

Life for young Muslim girls in Britain is often stricter than it would be in their country of origin, as parents are fearful that their daughters will become contaminated by western culture, especially in the sexual realm. There is always the fear of her becoming pregnant which would bring shame and dishonor on the family. This problem is serious, for it shows not only a basic distrust of women, but a distrust of British society which places a high premium on individual freedom. Mohammed Raza again suggests that such "oppression" can only turn them against the Muslim faith.[4]

Relative Freedom during Education

As girls go to school and through university they have a feeling of freedom. All the girls I interviewed said that boy-girl friendships, frowned upon outside of marriage in the Muslim community, are the norm. At the level of higher education Muslim girls behave in a similar way to their western counterparts, functioning within mixed sex groups, and rotating around pubs and cafes. Many of the girls I spoke to said they would not drink alcohol in pubs, but at parties would have a glass of wine.

Muslim girls are forming relationships across cultures. They are also forming friendships with young men of other racial groups. To the older women this is a source of anxiety and is considered unacceptable. It was very difficult to find out if these relationships are sexual relationships. It was admitted by about half the girls I interviewed that they knew Muslim young people who were in sexual relationships, their parents being totally unaware of it. Some girls said they believed that some Muslim young people were in boy-girl sexual relationships in very much the same way as young people from the white British community. They said that this was not unusual with those in higher education but was more common amongst the boys than the girls. The girls told me they were taught about contraception at school.

The girls I spoke to realised that their time of relative freedom would soon come to an end with marriage, and were making the most of this freedom. They said that many girls go on to further education only to prolong their time of freedom. All girls I interviewed indicated that if they wanted to do something a way could be found, and they would do it without their parents' knowledge. It is quite common for higher education students who live at home or stay with relatives (and the majority do) to say to their parents that they have late lectures or need to remain back to do work. Living in such a strict environment at home means they have to deceive their parents in order to have the freedoms they want. However, the relationships they form with young men are generally not going anywhere, as both partners know that they will be having an arranged marriage in the not so distant future. Coming from such a strict environment, when they start at university some Muslim young people find the first taste of freedom very sweet and go wild. They often behave in more extreme ways than their western counterparts.

Muhammad Anwar, in "Young Muslims in Britain", mentions a survey that was done in 1983 by the Commission for Racial Equality amongst young Muslims, both women and men. Fifty-three per cent of them wanted to arrange their own marriages. He says that the responses of those who expressed opposition to their marriage being arranged indicate that as Muslims grow up in Britain the system of arranging marriages will not work in its rigid form. This trend was confirmed when over 80% of young Muslims and over 70% of parents agreed that "parents want to keep the system of arranged marriages much more than their children do". He concludes that opposition to the system is increasing, and the attitudes of young people and examples of rebellion against arranged marriages indicate that this issue in future will lead to greater inter-generational conflict in the Muslim community.[5]

The Fear of Westernisation

The greatest fear that haunts the Muslim community is that the younger generation will become westernised, and will lose not only their cultural heritage, but also their religion. The fear is real, for Muslim youth is becoming westernised and secularised.[6] Christian parents likewise fear that their children will find their identity in secular culture and leave the Christian faith. Again, this is a real fear, as large numbers of young people leave the Church every year.

The process of westernisation, and other people's fear of it, is not confined to the young generation of Muslims. Older Muslim women who have started to go out to work have found this to be a cause of conflict within the home. Husbands fear that their wives will become westernised and want to wear western dress, and that they will develop relationships with men.

The Muslim community in the UK is a minority community, but in most cases its members have come from a situation where Islam had the majority status. Islam is used to functioning as a majority community and it has no *fiqh*, or teaching, as to functioning in a minority situation. In the UK there was no early thinking within Islam as how they should function in such a situation, and no reason to see the necessity for it. As a result, a generation of immigrants was brought up with no Qur'anic schools to attend, which means they often know very little if anything about their religion. This generation has been shaped by British schools and institutions, by globalisation, and television. They are contextually different from the older generation.

Factors Causing Contextual Change

One factor that encourages contextual change to take place is peer group pressure. Girls want to dress, look and behave in the same way as their British counterparts, to enable them to be part of the peer group and thus gain acceptance. In Britain many Muslim girls have two different wardrobes, one to be used for family and special events, and the other (hidden from the parents) for wearing outside of the home. Peer group pressure can also lead them into pre-marital sexual relationships, drugs, dating, dancing, alcohol and other activities common in the society in which they find themselves.

Another very significant factor that has brought contextual change is the educational system. Access of women to the British educational system has been the biggest factor in changing the position of women within Islam. The system shapes its pupils to have various thought patterns, promotes argument and analysis of ideologies, and operates within a cultural framework based on secularism. It has meant the desegregation of the sexes as well as the equality of them. This is the one factor that has brought the most conflict between generations and cultures, as it speaks of choice and individualism as opposed to the primacy of the community.

The workplace in a similar way has helped bring contextual change. When young Muslims go to work, their income determines their class in society and they will be defined within that class, sometimes adopting the attitudes and symbols of it. Even language can be a means of contextual change as speaking English gives access to literature and other media through which the culture and customs of British society can be imbibed. And then there is the society itself, its songs, its youth culture, its work ethic, its concept of relationships, the media and many more factors within it.

Identity

Linked to contextual change is the question of identity. How do young Muslims see themselves? Do they consider themselves Pakistani or Bangladeshi even though they were born in Britain, or do they consider themselves British? Do they see themselves as Muslims or with a wider ethnic tribal identity?

None of the young people I interviewed had any sentiment or loyalty to the home country of their parents. They considered themselves above all to be British. Half of the young girls identified with the broader Asian viewpoint. However, after the events of September 11, 2001, there was a redefining of Islam and Islamic identity. It is probably fair to say that most Muslim young people in Britain now see and identify themselves as British Muslim. Linked with this British Muslim identity has been an increase in the popularity of the *hijab,* which is seen as an expression of a woman's Muslim identity.

Conflict of Cultures

Muslim young people in Britain live in two cultures. There is the strict Muslim culture in their home and the Western, postmodern, culture in their schools and universities. There is therefore a cultural conflict going on in their lives, and this is more acute with Muslim girls because parents tend to be more protective of them over the issues of dating, sexuality and marriage. Whilst Muslim parents cling desperately to traditional ideals, their children grow up with different aspirations, which they know their parents will reject. The gap is sometimes unbridgeable and a double identity is inevitable. To guard the family's reputation, secrecy is essential.

One 19 year old Bengali girl describes how she leads a double life. At home she is the subservient daughter, but once outside she becomes a hipster-wearing, cigarette-smoking, trend-obsessed teenager. She says that to her parents she is the dutiful, obedient, wide-eyed, innocent daughter. "At home you won't catch me in low-cut tops or tight hipsters or smoking. Yet once I leave the front door, a sudden metamorphosis occurs. Off comes the straitjacket and out comes a creative, flirtatious, impetuous hip chick." Her father is a senior figure in London's Muslim Bengali community, and she is expected to behave accordingly. She says that sometimes she feels trapped and conscience stricken that she can't be open about the other side of her identity, but "I know it would break my parent's heart and cause scandal". So the sexy outfits she secretly owns remain hidden at the back of her wardrobe.[7]

This entrapment between two cultures is having a detrimental effect on the health of young Muslim girls, according to a paper presented at the British Psychological Society in 1997 by Dev Sharma (psychologist, Newham Council) and Dr David Jones (Birkbeck College, London University). The study was conducted because of the rise in the number of Muslim teenage girls experiencing emotional problems and behavioural difficulties. The report states that Muslims girls are very anxious and are up to three times more likely to harm themselves than their white counterparts, either as a cry for help or in a suicide attempt. It reports that there is enormous pressure for them to conform to cultural patterns, especially when it comes to sexual morals and friendships between boys and girls. However if parents are overprotective children are more likely to rebel.

A recent report by the Safer Surrey Partnership Team (funded and supported by Surrey County Council, Surrey Police and the Metropolitan Police Service) exploring the multiple and changing identities of young Pakistani women and their needs in the UK, said that there is a clear indication that the problem of suicides and attempted suicides is particularly acute amongst this group of women. This group had been found to be characterised by higher rates than their counterparts amongst the white population or within other ethnic groups. Factors identified as contributing to this pattern included submission and deference to men and elders, the continued prevalence of forced (as opposed to arranged) marriages, and financial problems associated with the payment of dowries. Stress therefore appears to be closely related to the clash of cultures. It is only after girls take drastic action, such as running away from home or attempting suicide, that a problem is recognised at all. The report also said that it is possible that the situation is aggravated by a certain "freezing" of the cultural norms that were prevalent at the time when the majority of their parents migrated to the UK. These cultural norms have not evolved according to the trajectories which might have been expected in their country of origin. It is also possible that this "freezing" of cultural norms and the increased pressure placed on girls to ensure that these norms are maintained has happened because the parents' generation is struggling to protect its sense of community and cultural identity in the face of the dominant English culture and racism.[8]

Patriarchal Structures

From the time of birth girls are considered a liability, as they will leave the family home and get married. Their birth can go unannounced and condolences can be offered. A boy is what is desirable and his birth is given more importance, as he is an asset that will carry on the family name and inheritance. Boys are considered a capital investment for economic reasons.[9] This belief emanates from the patriarchal structure of village societies, and conflicts with

British culture and law where both sexes are considered equally important and independent.

Religion and Young People

Adherence to Islam is at a low ebb with many young Muslim people, as they have embraced the secularism of the society in which they live in the UK. In spite of this they still consider themselves to be Muslims. Some young people do have their own views about Islam but feel they are marginalised, and have been ignored. One reason for this is that a generation has grown up untaught in Islam, as in the majority of areas there were no Qur'anic schools. When their parents' generation came as new immigrants to Britain, all the social structures of the society had to be put into place and Qur'anic schools were not prioritised. This has been rectified in the last few years, and probably all Muslim children would now attend mosque instruction after school on several days a week for two to three hours. Children as young as four can be seen going for this instruction.

Another reason for young people's lack of interest in Islam could be the way in which their parents have communicated the faith to them. Parents tend to transmit to their children their own particular customs, ways and interpretations of practising the Islamic system. These customs apparently have a high rejection level by the younger generation.[10] Raza, writing in 1991 believed that the Muslim community had failed the younger generation because they themselves hold "reactionary and obscurantist" views of Islam. These in some cases may be a result of traditional, rural backgrounds in their countries of origin, whereas their children may have a much more intellectual, urban and international outlook. Specifically, he claimed, the community had failed to create an attractive Islamic environment, or make mosques into community centres where the younger generation could meet other Muslims socially. He believed that the older generation had not been able to define Islamic values and standards in a clear-cut manner, or suggest alternative Islamic ways of meeting young people's needs.[11] In the last few years, since 1997-98, this has changed and Muslim religious leaders have started programmes for young people at mosques and community centres.

All the women and girls I interviewed (except for two girls from Saudi Arabia) had thought very little about their religion. One of the girls I interviewed was very fearful that I would ask her questions on Islam, as she admitted she knew nothing about it. One of the major reasons for this was the lack of teaching received by the girls.

It is only now that Islam is beginning to contextualise itself in certain areas to the situation in Britain. It is providing places for women in all new mosques, sometimes very large sections and alongside the section for the men. This is a new development. There are now teaching and prayer groups on Islam for young people in some community centres, similar to house groups in the Christian context.

Alongside this disinterest in Islam there is the opposite phenomenon of a growing number of young girls who are being radicalised with Islamic fervour. They are veiling according to the strictest Islamic code and taking their religion very seriously. One example of this would be Shabina Begum who took her school to court in May 2004, claiming her human rights had been breached because she was not allowed to wear the all-concealing *jilbab to* school. The school, whose uniform includes an outfit approved by Islamic scholars for Muslim students, felt that allowing one pupil to wear a more extreme form of covering would put pressure on other Muslims girls by implying they were insufficiently observant. Shabina Begum lost her case and now attends a Muslim school.

Conclusion

Life in Britain is bringing contextual changes within the Muslim community and as a result there are changes in the position of Muslim women and girls. It is most noticeable in the second-generation girls who have been born in this country. However this new freedom, which is a very limited freedom, is bringing considerable stress and tension between generations. As well as a generational gap there is now a cultural divide. For example, parents think it is their right to choose their children's partner in marriage and the children think it is their right to choose for themselves. The traditional Muslim ideas are in direct conflict with the aspirations and desires of the younger generation. There is now a cultural conflict between the generations.

The older generation cannot understand the younger generation who appear to them to be throwing off all the traditions of the past and becoming westernised. This contextualisation is spoken of by the younger generation as a redefinement of Islam. With this cultural redefinement they want a religious redefinement. They look on Islam as being something that is rooted in the generation of older holy men who seem unable to understand or accommodate them.

Education

Muslim women are fighting back and their principal weapon is education. Education is playing a large part in empowering Muslim women. In many Muslim countries, notably Iran and Saudi Arabia and Kuwait women form a majority of university students. Thousands of Muslim women are now doctors, lawyers, bankers, architects etc, and worldwide there are now playwrights, novelists, film-makers, police, T.V. presenters and in Iran and Turkey even fighter pilots.

It is as they are educated at university that they are able to take their place in society and realise their rights. But they still face enormous handicaps, such as inequality in the workplace. They claim that there is hostility from college, discrimination at work and struggles within their communities.[1] Muslim girls do face a disproportionate amount of pressure from their immediate family, who are often unwilling to support their daughter's career aspirations out of fear as to how this will be perceived in the wider community. It is twice as hard for them to succeed. However a change is being detected in parental attitudes towards girls and work. One of the possible reasons for this shift is identified as the realisation among Muslim parents that educational capital is necessary for survival, and that Muslim men increasingly are looking for more educated partners.

Honor and Shame

The most difficult problem facing the Muslim community in Britain is that of male/female relationships. Modernity encourages desegregation which, for the parents, leads to confusion and anxiety. Muslim parents' fear for their daughters is easy to understand when we look at the sexual language and images with which our culture has become saturated.

Traditional Muslim society does not function on the basis of individualism but on the basis of community. This is why the dictates of the community are so important. The community is more important than the individual. Therefore an important issue is whether Islam and the community can change its concept of women from being a liability and guarding them, to a position where they can be considered of equal value to men.

At present the community continues to dictate how women should behave, and appears to have little accommodation for cultural change. Not to adhere to the dictates of the community brings shame. To prevent this shame, the family exerts both open and subtle pressure to make their daughters conform. To change this situation would need a change in the concepts of honor and shame and how women are viewed, but this would be a major paradigm shift.

Women would need to be viewed as an asset to the family, and as people who can be trusted to take responsibility for their own lives and moral behaviour. Men's attitude and behaviour towards women would also need to change. At present men can have extra-marital affairs and are free to do many things which, if done by a woman, would bring disgrace. Whereas the concept of right and wrong as we understand it applies to actions, regardless of who carries them out, the concept of shame seems to be attached to a far greater degree to women's actions than to men's. It is not a level playing field, and this balance needs to be readdressed. This is one of the single biggest factors affecting the position of women.

There are young Muslim women who want the freedoms of their British counterparts in all aspects of their lives. Many of these young girls are frightened to speak out but there is an increasing band that finds the courage to do so. It is in desperation that they stand up for their rights and freedoms, fully aware of the alternative. They look at their mothers and are determined to live what they consider to be a better life, where they are able to pursue careers, choose their own marriage partners, and live a life of what they consider to be freedom. To do this, however, means breaking away from the pressures of the community and often the family.

Women and Jihad

Since 2000 there has been a steady progression of suicide attacks carried out by women in areas of conflict. This growing use of women on suicide missions by Islamist groups is significant because it flies in the face of the deeply held religious belief that women should not take part in fighting. Jihad for the woman is considered to be taking part in the Hajj. This use of women as *shaheeds* (martyrs) is a new-found pool of womanpower.

Women and Modernity

The position of women in Islam is largely dependant on the degree to which Islam can embrace modernity. Some believe that women should not play any part in the development of nations or religion. If this attitude prevails, Muslim nations risk missing out on the potential contribution of 50% of their populations. If Muslims isolate women, then their effectiveness will be reduced considerably. The more radically Islamic a society becomes, the more there tends to be deterioration in the position of women and the more their rights are denied. The more liberal a Muslim society becomes, the more rights women have.

The problem facing the Muslim community today is how to be both modern and Muslim. The difficulty is that many Muslims perceive modernity as synonymous with secularism, which is seen in a very negative light. They look at the post-modern secular society of the West and do not want to be identified with it. They see the breakdown of the family and of society and consider it to be morally corrupt. Some do say that it is impossible – and undesirable – for Islam to accept modernity.

The increase in travel and communications has brought modern thinking to many parts of the Muslim world. In Islam there is no central religious authority, equivalent for example to the role of the Vatican in the Roman Catholic Church. The Muslim modernists today are not the clerics, they are the professionals, many of whom are western-educated but dislike the moral laxity of the West. These modernists are convinced that Islam need not adhere to the canons of the 11th century, and argue that much of Islamic law was adapted by man and not ordained by God. What they are looking for are reforms that are authentically Islamic and yet modern. The modernists face opposition from clerics on one hand and the radical Islamic groups on the other. What they are really calling for is a renewal of the spirit of Islam by applying it to the society of the day.

Some modernists are calling for a return to the fundamental message of Islam that was given at Mecca and which emphasised the dignity of all human beings. They claim that this message was replaced by a set of sexist, racist and repressive decrees that later became cemented into Islamic Law.[2]

Other modern thinkers say that Islam should be the moral basis of a modern and progressive society but that it could not approve everything done in the name of modernisation. Their point of view is that Islam should act as a restraining principle, allowing the Muslim community to adopt European ideas and sciences without abandoning Islam itself.[3] An example of this would be the writer Akbar S Ahmed, who asks the question about the clash between Islam and the West: how can Muslims learn to understand and respect the values of Western society without compromising their own central beliefs and practices.[4] This is the struggle that Islam is having at this moment with the modern world. Muslim thinkers find it difficult to separate modernism (which is acceptable) from westernisation (which is not) and again tied to this is the position of women. The more traditional religious values are idolised for political ends, the greater the dysfunction in the status of women.[5]

The Patriarchal Society

It can be argued that it is the patriarchal nature of society in Muslim-majority countries that is responsible for the inferior position of women in those countries (or originating from those countries), and not Islam. Certainly there are great differences in the status of women across the Muslim world, and indeed between different regions and classes of women within nations. These are partly attributable to cultural differences. But this argument is weak, as Islam has helped to shape those societies over the centuries, reinforcing patriarchal practices by giving them the sanction of religion.

As we saw in chapter two, the parameters of Islam were strongly influenced by the context of the patriarchal society in which they were being defined, and the cultural norms of that time became embedded as part of the religion. The position and view of women thus defined is set out in the Qur'an and the Hadith. It is difficult to say what is cultural and what is Islamic, as in Islam the culture, society and religion cannot easily be separated. Islam is an all embracing system.

The Future

There are youth groups being started throughout the country called Young Muslims UK which include cells with women. These groups are rooted in the contemporary situation and are trying to address the contextual change that is taking place. There is also a move to contextualise Islam by personalising it, or in other words making it a personal faith rather than a community faith. It is believed that personalising and internalising Islam would give the strength to withstand the forces of postmodernity and secularism.

One extremely important factor that could make a difference is racism. The British Muslim community of young people expects to be accepted on an equal basis to the white community. The lack of this acceptance could drive these young people back into a conservative Islam. The feeling that they are being treated with unfair suspicion by the police as potential terrorists, and portrayed as such in sections of the media, are examples of the kind of lack of acceptance that can have the effect of radicalising young Muslims.

Another factor is whether the British Muslim male can and will want to cope with a Muslim girl who has become western and modern, or whether in the end it will be destructive to the marriage and family situation.

Progressive Muslims have clear views on future direction Islam should take regarding the rights of women. "Progressive Muslims begin with a simple yet radical stance that the Muslim community as a whole cannot achieve justice unless justice is guaranteed for Muslim women. There can be no progressive interpretation of Islam without gender justice. Gender equality is a measuring stick for the broader concerns of social justice and pluralism. It is imperative to conceive women's rights as human rights."[6]

Not all Muslim commentators are optimistic that such change will be easily achieved.

"It's a struggle all the way for women: a struggle against orthodoxy, a struggle against certain oppressive cultural norms, which do not permit women to enter certain fields. As women assert their rights to find a place of honor in the society, the society, which is under the domination of men, reacts quite sharply and tries to put more restrictions over them. This struggle will go on for a long time to come."[7]

Update: Five Years Later and it's a Different World

In the last five years the world has become a radically different place. The watershed was 9/11, with the ensuing years resulting in the transformation of societies. Islam became the focal point in many arenas in a bid to become centre stage and powerful. In all spheres it now wanted its voice and presence to be recognised and heard.

Islamic Identity

In the UK there has been a complete turnaround in regard to Islamic identity and how Muslims perceive themselves. Many of the first Muslim immigrants did not speak English well, but were desperate to assimilate, driven in part by the desire for work and prosperity.[8] A recent survey conducted in the UK by NOP for Channel Four Dispatches revealed some startling results. Immigrants have usually tended to become more secular and less religious than their parents by the second generation. But the survey shows Muslims have gone in precisely the opposite direction.

Today's young British Muslims are less liberal and more devout than their parents. Their beliefs render many of them determined not just to be different but also to be separate from the rest of the nation. Muslim integration into British Society has effectively come to a halt. The evidence that integration has stopped comes from comparing this survey with previous studies, most notably one conducted in 1993 by Tariq Modood, professor of sociology at Bristol University who says political identification with Islam has grown disproportionately among the young since then.[9]

Muslims are now more conscious of the worldwide Islamic

identity or *umma,* an attitude which was intensified since the wars in Iraq and Afghanistan. They are now loyal to this trans-national identity above their own national identities and nations. As the individual in Islam is not important, the communities gain their strength and power by being represented in numbers united by their Islamic identity.

Modernisation and Islam

There is no discussion in the Muslim world on the position and rights of women. Not one constitution in the Muslim world upholds sexual equality. But there have been gains in Tunisia and Morocco where women are being given more rights.

Morocco's young, western-educated king, Mohammed VI, opened a session of Parliament in 2004 with a dramatic question: "How can society achieve progress, while women, who represent half the nation, see their rights violated and suffer as a result of injustice, violence and marginalisation?" The king proposed radical changes to the laws that govern the family. He virtually banned polygamy by instituting a system whereby the husband had to get permission from his wife or wives and then go before a judge to argue a case on the necessity of a second wife. Before this ruling the man could divorce his wife simply by uttering the prescribed words; now the decision will be made by a judge. Women can initiate a divorce. It is in the cities of Morocco that these new laws have made a difference, to the injustices suffered by women and children.[10]

Women, *Shari'a* and the West

Many Muslims in the West would like to see a formal link between state law and *Shari'a,* particularly in the realm of family law. There have been many calls for various aspects of *Shari'a* to be incorporated into the civil laws of western countries. Muslim communities believe that they need to live under their own laws which are determined by their religion, rather than the laws imposed upon them. However *Shari'a* discriminates against women. The difficulty is that western governments, not realising the implications of *Shari'a* will be swayed to allow their presence within the Muslim communities. In the UK the government has already introduced *Shari'a* compliant pensions and mortgages. *Shari'a* is also present by default, in the form of *Shari'a* marriages, divorces, wills and polygamy. Muslim women are facing increasing discrimination in respect of these issues.

Other Muslim scholars, such as the influential Sheik Yusuf al-Qaradawi argue that western governments must make their laws more in line with *Shari'a*. This pressure is bearing fruit. In the US and UK, for instance, the government employs *Shari'a* advisors in various departments. The UK has used *fatwas* to gain Muslim support for organ donations. Schools have introduced *halal* food (sometimes for all pupils irrespective of their faith), segregated sports and Muslim dress and head coverings. Muslim chaplains, Muslim prayer rooms, *halal* food and Muslim headcoverings have also been accepted in a variety of public services such as the police and the prison service. Local councils are now considering *Shari'a* principles in their decisions on housing, education, health and other matters. In June 2006, Britain's Home Office withdrew proposed legislation banning forced marriages, apparently for fear of antagonizing the Muslim community. With all of this being implemented the position of women in the West deteriorates.

All this has impacted women: increasing numbers are wearing the veil, whatever form it takes, either of their own free will or as a result of being forced to wear it through family and community pressure. The compulsory wearing of the veil is fast becoming the norm. In

Islamic schools and in many state schools Muslim girls are well-covered and all wear the *hijab*. There is a difficulty with swimming lessons for girls at school and the community is now asking for separate times for Muslim girls to participate in swimming. Many parents are refusing to allow their daughters to attend swimming lessons. A special bathing suit has been designed for them that totally cover all parts of the body. Such restrictions on activities and the imposition of Islamic clothing makes women responsible for the sexual responses of men. Femininity is seen as a threat.

As communities feel they are pressured they retreat within themselves and women will find it increasing difficult to exercise any self-expression or freedom of movement or choice. There will be more fracturing of families as girls seeking the freedom of their British counterparts, will have to choose between freedom and family risking possible death in honor killings. As society polarises, the rules of honor and shame will be intensified. Islam is a man's world and continues to be so, and the old rules of honor and shame are becoming even more important. It is the women and the girls who will always pay the price.

References

Introduction

1. 2001 UK Census official figures.
2. Ibid.
3. Kenneth Leech, The Eye of the Storm (London: Darton, Longman and Todd, 1992), p. 147.
4. Raymond Lee, Doing Research on Sensitive Topics (London: Sage Publications, 1993), p. 4.
5. Ibid., p. 101.
6. Ibid., p. 76.
7. Ibid., p. 79.

Chapter 1

1. J.Spencer Trimingham, Christianity among the Arabs in Pre-Islamic Times (Beirut: Librairie du Liban, 1990), p. 308.
2. W Robertson-Smith, Kinship and Marriage in Early Arabia, (London: Adam and Charles Black, 1903), p. 145-46.
3. Ibid., p. 80.
4. Fatima Mernissi, Beyond the Veil (Bloomington, IN: Indiana University Press, 1987), p. 70.
5. Gertrude Stern, Marriage in Early Islam (London: The Royal Asiatic Society, 1939), p. 70.
6. Robertson-Smith, Kinship and Marriage in Early Arabia, p. 93.
7. Mazhar Ul Haq Khan, Purdah and Polygamy (Peshwar: Taraqiyet, 1972), p. 13.
8. Anwar Hekmat, Women and the Koran (New York: Prometheus, 1997), p. 102.
9. Mernissi, Beyond the Veil, p. 67.

10. Zakaria Bashier, The Makkan Crucible (Leicester: The Islamic Foundation, 1991), p. 48, quoting Ibn Hisham, pp. 155-7.

11. Mernissi, Beyond the Veil, p. 69, quoting Ibn Saad, Kitab al-Tabaqat al-Kubra, Vol. 8, p. 95.

12. Maxime Rodinson, Mohammed (Harmondsworth: Penguin, 1971), p. 42.

13. Bashier, The Makkan Crucible, pp. 52-4.

14. Asghar Ali Engineer, The Rights of Women in Islam (Selangor Darul Ehsan: IBS Buku Sdn Bhd, 1992), pp. 21-2.

15. Stern, Marriage in Early Islam, p. 62.

16. Mohammad Marmaduke Pickthall (trans.), The Meaning of the Glorious Qur'an (Birmingham: UK Islamic Mission Dawah Centre, 1997), p. 89.

17. Hekmat, Women and the Koran, pp. 41-2.

18. Robertson-Smith, Kinship and Marriage, p. 291.

19. Ibid., p. 293.

20. DS Margoliouth, Mohammed (London & New York: G.P.Putnam's Sons, 1906), p. 29.

21. Fatima Mernissi, Women and Islam (Oxford: Blackwell, 1991), p. 120, quoting Tabari, Tafsir, Vol. 8, p. 107.

22. Ibid., p. 116.

23. Emile Dermengham, The Life of Mahomet (London: George Routledge & Sons, 1930), p. 44.

24. Mernissi, Women and Islam, p. 116.

25. Hekmat, Women and the Koran, p. 38.

26. Margoliouth, Mohammed, p. 30.

27. Engineer, The Rights of Women, pp. 32-3.

28. Mernissi, Women and Islam, p. 4, quoting Mohammed Arafa The Rights of Women in Islam.

29. Ibid., p. 37.

30. Ibid., p. 5.

31. Ibid., p. 49-50.

32. Ibid., pp. 6-7.

Chapter 2

1. All quotations from the Qur'an unless otherwise stated are from Mohammad Marmaduke Pickthall (trans.), The Meaning of the Glorious Qur'an.

2. Ibid., Sura 4:1.

3. Ibid., Sura 49:13.

4. Ibid., Sura 17:70.

5. Murtada Mutahhari, The Rights of Women in Islam (Tehran: World Organization for Islamic Services, 1981), p. 126.

6. Abdul-Ghaffar Hasan, The Rights and Duties of Women in Islam (London: Al-Qur'an Society, 1992), p. 5.

7. Amina Wadud-Muhsin, Qur'an and Woman (Kuala Lumpur: Penerbit Fajar Bakti Sdn Bhd, 1992), p. 7.

8. Qur'an, Sura 33:35.

9. Leila Ahmed, Women and Gender in Islam (New Haven, CT: Yale University Press, 1992), p. 65.

10. Ibid., p. 66.

11. Sahih Al Bukhari in The Alim (Silver Spring, Maryland: ISL Software Corp, 1986-1999), Hadith 1:301.

12. Ibid., Hadith 8:456.

13. Ibid., Hadiths 1:28, 2:161, 2:541, 4:464, 7:124, 7:125, 7:126, 8:555.

14. P Newton & M Haqq, Women in Islam (Warley: TMFMT, 1993), p. 13.

15. Sunan Abu-Dawood, Hadith 876 narrated by Qays ibn Sa'd.

16. Hekmat, Women and the Koran, p. 90.

17. Qur'an, Sura 36:56.

18. Sahih Al Bukhari, Hadith 161:2.

19. Amin Qasim, The Liberation of Women (New York: The American University in Cairo Press, 1992), p. 11.

20. Sahih Al Bukhari. Hadith 1:28.

21. Qur'an, Sura 4:34.

22. N.J.Dawood (trans.), The Koran (Harmondsworth: Penguin, 1983), Sura 4:34.

23. Wadud-Muhsin, Qur'an and Women, p. 7.

24. Mohammed Zafeeruddin Nadvi, Modesty and Chastity in Islam (Kuwait: Islamic Book Publishers, 1982), p. 160.

25. Qur'an, Sura 4:34.

26. Nadvi, Modesty and Chastity, p. 160.

27. Hekmat, Women and the Koran, p. 215.

28. Sahih, Al-Bukhari, Hadith 121:7.

29. Sahih, Al-Tirmidhi, Hadith 959.

30. Qortobi, commenting on Qur'an 30:21

31. Newton & Haqq, Women in Islam, p. 22, quoting Ihy'a 'Uloum ed-Din by Ghazali, Dar al-Kotob al-'Elmeyah, Beirut, Vol. II, Kitab Adab al-Nikah, p. 52.

32. Qur'an, Sura 2:282.

33. Sahih Al-Bukhari, Hadith 301:1.
34. Qur'an, Sura 4:11.
35. Asghar Ali Engineer, Islam, Women and Gender Justice (New Delhi: Gyan Publishing House, 2001), p. 40.
36. Qur'an, Sura 24:31.
37. Qasim, The Liberation of Women, p. 39.
38. Ibid., p. 42.
39. Ibid., p. 42.
40. Shahla Heiri, "Obedience versus Autonomy", in Martin E Marty & R Scott Appleby (eds.), Fundamentalisms and Society (Chicago: University of Chicago Press, 1993), pp. 185-6.
41. Ibid.
42. Ibid.
43. Dawood, The Koran, Sura 4:3.
44. Dawood, The Koran, Sura 4:129.
45. Hekmat, Women and the Koran, pp 129-30.
46. Qur'an, Sura 4:20.

Chapter 3

1. Roland Muller, Honor and Shame (Philadelphia, PA: Xlibris Corporation, 2000), p. 46-8.
2. Ibid., p81.
3. Judy Mabro & El Solh Camilla Fawzi (eds.), Muslim Women's Choices (Oxford: Berg Publishers, 1994), p. 8.
4. Ibid., p. 137.
5. Mohammad S Raza, Islam in Britain, (Leicester: Volcano Press Ltd, 1991), p. 88.
6. Ibid., p. 86.
7. Jamila Brilbhushan, Women in Purdah and Out of It (New Delhi: Vikas, 1980), p. 47.
8. Bo Utas (ed.), Women in Islamic Societies (London: Curzon Press, 1983), p. 6.
9. Mabro & El Solh Muslim Women's Choices, p. 153.
10. Utas, Women in Islamic Societies, p. 5.
11. Sahih Muslim in The Alim (Silver Spring, Maryland: ISL Software Corp, 1986-99), Hadith 672.
12. Lisa Beyer, "The Price of Honor", Time, Jan 18, 1999, p. 29.
13. "In the Name of the Father", Asianwoman, Sept 2000, p. 20.

14. "UK Muslims Condemn Honor Killings", BBC News, Sept 30, 2003, at http://news.bbc.co.uk/1/hi/england/london/3150142.stm., viewed, April 15, 2008.

15. Ibid.

16. Lewis Smith, "A Murderous Clash of Culture", The Sunday Times, Oct 5, 2003, p. 9.

17. David Jones, "As Yet Another Failed Father is Jailed for an Honor Killing", Daily Mail, Oct 9, 2003, pp. 48-9.

18. Smith, "A Murderous Clash of Culture", p. 9.

19. Suna Erdem, "Honor Suicides:death by a bullet in the back", The Times, May 25, 2006, p. 45.

Chapter 4

1. Shagufta Yaqub, "Forced to Eat the Forbidden Fruit", Q-News, Jan 1998, p. 12.

2. Abi Newman, "That Can Only End in Tears", Newham Recorder, Aug 29, 2001, p. 97.

3. "Forced Marriages Causing Concern", BBC News, March 22, 2004, at http://news.bbc.co.uk/1/hi/scotland/3557727.stm., viewed, April 15, 2008.

4. "Guidance Tackles Forced Marriages", BBC News, March 31, 2004, at http://news.bbc.co.uk/1/hi/uk/3585289.stm., viewed, April 15, 2008.

5. "Lawyers ignore forced marriages", BBC News, March 29, 2004, at http://news.bbc.co.uk/1/hi/uk/3576755.stm., viewed, April 15, 2008.

6. Steve Boggan, "Bounty Hunters Tail Runaway Brides", The Independent, July 20, 1998, p. 3.

7. Steve Boggan & Peter Popham, "The Arrangement", The Independent, July 21, 1998, Tuesday Review, p. 1.

8. Richard Ford, "Judge annuls Girl's Forced Marriage",The Times, July 6, 2006, p. 25.

9. Newman, "That Can Only End in Tears", p.97.

10. Nicola Woolcock, "Britain Rescues 100 Men from Forced Marriages", The Times, March 6, 2004, p. 8.

11. Chris Brooke, "In-Laws Turned a Blind Eye to Bride's Murder", Daily Mail, Feb.6, 2008. p. 39.

12. Forbidden Love, broadcast February 1998, 9.30pm, by BBC.

13. Tim Raymond, "Star-Cross'd Couple Risk Death for Love", The Sunday

Times, Jan 23, 1994, p. 5.

14. Richard Ford & Alexandra Frean, "Fears of Sexual Freedom Lead to Forced Marriages", The Times, Nov 13, 2002.

15. "Couple's Story", British Muslims Monthly Survey, Oct 1997, Vol. 5, No. 10, p. 5.

16. Mark McCrum, "At Last We Can Stop Running", The Sunday Times, May 21, 2006, News Review p. 11.

17. Boggan, "Bounty Hunters", p. 3.

18. Warren Hodge, "Deadly Affair", International Herald Tribune, Oct 20, 1997, p. 1.

19. Bill A Musk, Touching the Soul of Islam, (Crowborough: Marc, 1995), pp. 69-70.

20. Phil & Julie Parshall, Lifting the Veil (Waynesboro, GA: Gabriel Publishing, 2002), pp. 158-9, quoting Musk & Peters.

21. James Chapman, "Women get *virginity fix* NHS operations in Muslim-driven trend." Daily Mail, Nov 7, 2007.

22. Zubeida Malik, "Polygamy Law Set for Challenge", BBC News, June 18, 2000, at http://news.bbc.co.uk/1/hi/uk/791263.stm, viewed, April 15, 2008.

23. Ibid.

24. "Polygamy in Britain", Islam for Today, at http//:www.islamfortoday. com/polygamy.1 htm., viewed, April 15, 2008.

Chapter 5

1. "Why Older Women are Divorcing", The Sunday Times, March, 2002.

2. Aina Khan, "Bigamy Warning for UK Muslims", BBC News, Feb 23, 2001, at http://news.bbc.co.uk/1/hi/uk/1185459.stm., viewed April 15, 2008.

3. Ibid.

4. Fauzia Ahmad, "Untying the Knot", Q-News, Dec 2003, No. 352.

5. Tania Branigan, "Islamic Weddings Leave Women Unprotected", The Guardian, Nov 24, 2003.

6. Aina Khan, "Viewpoint: Women and Shari'ah Law", BBC News, Oct 22, 2003.

7. "Domestic Violence in the Muslim Community", Q-News, June 1999.

8. Ibid.

9. Ibid.

10. "A Question of Honor", The Independent UK, 10th Feb, 2008

11. Ibid.
12. Claire Coleman, "A Degree of Duplicity", Daily Mail, 11 April, 2005, p46-47.
13. Ibid.
14. Ibid.
15. Muhammad Anwar, Young Muslims in Britain (Leicester: The Islamic Foundation, 1994), p. 33.
16. Yaqub, "Forced to Eat the Forbidden Fruit", p. 9.
17. Ibid.
18. Ibid.
19. Anwar, Young Muslims, p. 25.
20. "Tougher Penalties for Genital Mutilation", The Guardian, March 3, 2004.

Chapter 6

1. Mostafa Hashem Sherif, "What is Hijab", The Muslim World, 77, July-Oct 1987, Nos. 3-4, pp. 151-2.
2. Abdul Rahman Adullah (ed.), Islamic Dress Code for Women (Riyadh: Darussalam, 1999), p. 9.
3. Helen Hardacre, "The Impact of Fundamentalisms on Women, the Family and Interpersonal Relations", in Martin E Marty & R Scott Appleby (eds.), Fundamentalisms and Society (Chicago: University of Chicago Press, 1993), p. 146.
4. "Inside Afghanistan: Behind the Veil", BBC News, June 27, 2001, at http://news.bbc.co.uk/1/hi/world/south_asia/1410061.stm, viewed 15 April 2008.
5. Yasmin Alibhai-Brown, "Muslim Women's Struggle to Wear What They Like", The Independent, June 23, 2003, p. 13.
6. Abdullah, Islamic Dress Code, p. 34.
7. Zawan, Al-Said, "Why I Won't Wear the Hijab", The Times, Feb 12, 2004, p. 3.
8. Ibid.
9. Alibhai-Brown, "Muslim Women's Struggle to Wear What They Like", p. 13.
10. Ibid.
11. Hardacre, "The Impact of Fundamentalisms", p. 145.
12. Ibid.
13. Ibid.
14. Natasha Walter, "When the Veil Means Freedom", The Guardian, Jan 20, 2004.

15. Alibhai-Brown, "Muslim Women's Struggle", p. 13.
16. Nasr Abu Azyd, "Religion and Secularism: From Polarization to Negotiation", in The Hague Centre of Initiatives of Change, Islam, Muslims and the West, Feb 11 2004.
17. Janice Turner, "What must Iran Make of this Free Woman", The Times, March 31, 2007.
18. Frances Childs, "A Lesson in Common Sense",Daily Mail, March 22, 2007, p 65.
19. Yasmin Alibhai-Brown, "The Brutal Truth that Hides Inside the Burka", Evening Standard.
20. Yasmin Alibhai-Brown, "Is it Time the Burka was banned in Britain", The Week, Jan 7, 2006, pp. 36-7.

Chapter 7

1. Raza, Islam in Britain, p. 84.
2. Ibid., p. 88.
3. Ibid., p. 87.
4. Ibid., p. 85.
5. Anwar, Young Muslims, p. 28.
6. Raza, Islam in Britain, p. 75.
7. Anjana Ahuja, "Caught in the Culture Trap", The Times, April 8, 1997, p. 14.
8. Salma Sulaimani, The Multiple and Changing Identities of Young Pakistani Women in Woking, Safer Surrey Partnership Team (Woking, 2000), p. 2.
9. Raza, Islam in Britain, p. 85.
10. Nimat Hafez Barazangi, 'Acculturation of North American Arab Muslims: Minority Relations or Worldview Variation?', Journal of Muslim Minority Affairs, July 1990, No. XIII, pp. 373-9.
11. Raza, Islam in Britain, p. 81.

Chapter 8

1. "Women Finding it Twice as Hard to Succeed", Q-News, Jan 1998, p. 9.
2. Peter Waldman, "Some Muslim Thinkers Want to Reinterpret Islam for Modern Times", Wall Street Journal, March 16, 1995, p. 10.
3. Derek Hopwood, "The Culture of Modernity in Islam and the Middle East", in John Cooper, Ronald Nettler & Mohammed Mahmoud (eds.), Islam and Modernity (London: I.B. Tauris, 1998), p 6.

4. Akbar S Ahmed, Living Islam (London: BBC Books, 1993), p. 19.
5. Mohammed Arkoun, Rethinking Islam (Boulder, CO: Westview, 1994), p. 62.
6. Omid Safa, "What is Progressive Islam", ISIM Newsletter, Dec 13, 2003, p. 48.
7. Engineer, Women and Gender Justice, p. 11.
8. Jon Snow, "Muslim Integration has come to a Halt", The Times, 6 Aug, 2006.
9. Ibid.
10. Nicola Fell, "Why a Young King is taking Morocco into a Feminist Future", The Sunday Herald, 29 Feb, 2004.

Subject Index by Chapter

Subject Index

Epilogue

The basis of this book was a Masters dissertation written for an Oxford college. It was completed in 1998, a time when very little was known about Islam in Britain and how it was conducting itself in the West. There was only sparse information coming from the Muslim community and no issues were surfacing. However, after 9/11 everything changed, the Muslim community came under scrutiny and issues relating to them began to grip the headlines.

When I submitted the completed dissertation to the college in 1998, there was no indication of what lay ahead. I received a phone call from the college saying that they didn't believe that I had written the dissertation myself and that they wanted me to change my position on Islam. To me it seemed unbelievable that they should think that someone else had written it, and that I should be asked to change my position on Islam when our universities prided themselves on neutrality of research. There was much correspondence between myself and the college but to no avail. Finally I wrote to the Vice-Chancellor of Oxford University and complained. They convened a court where I had to state my case. I had to take witnesses from our staff as I discovered that they believed it was written by the research department of our work -The Institute for the Study of Islam and Christianity. Then I had to argue for the neutrality of research.

When the judgement came they upheld my integrity in every way but still stated I had to change my position on Islam. After a visit to the college they wrote to me saying that whereas everyone would be expected to pass on a rewrite they could not guarantee that they would ever pass me. I took the dissertation and walked away. They awarded me a post-graduate Diploma in Theology.

It was to be four years before I could even look at my dissertation again, and then I took it out of the attic and turned it into a book. At the same time I updated it to be current to 2004.

It was a time of considerable stress. It was a dissertation ahead of its time, and everything I wrote about is today in the public arena. I am not the only person who has been asked to change their position on Islam with regard to a dissertation in our universities. I have known others who have faced the same fate with regard to doctoral and masters dissertations, and we will not be the last. In our universities it is now very difficult to be able to analyse and critique Islam. The day of free speech and neutrality of research is closing.

However I can look back now and know that I probably would never have embarked on writing books, if this episode had not happened in my life. In the end the glory goes to the Lord for His ways are perfect.

Books By the Same Author

Why Christian Women Convert to Islam

Why are hundreds of evangelical Christian women converting to Islam every year?

Many women are finding their daughters and granddaughters are becoming friendly with Muslim men. What these women don't realize, is that Islamic culture does not permit casual friendships across the sexes as we have in western countries. Many of these friendships will end in marriage.

What happens after these young women get married? Western culture and Islamic culture, Christianity and Islam have completely different world views. Christian girls do not realize that when they marry they will normally have to give up their faith and convert to Islam. Their children will have to be brought up as Muslims. They will also lose their freedom as an individual as they will in effect be marrying a family and a community.

This book explores these and many other issues relating to the interaction and marriage between Christian women and Muslim men.

A must read book for every mother and grandmother, even those who believe that it could never happen within their family. It is also an essential read for every pastor and church leader, and suitable for giving to those about to marry a Muslim or convert to Islam.